Rituals

To EMILY-
Best
Wishes!

Rituals

Joel Silverman

Doce Blant Publishing

www.DoceBlantPublishing.com

RITUALS

By Joel Silverman
Copyright ©2020 by Joel Silverman

All rights reserved.

Published by
Doce Blant Publishing, Federal Way, WA, 98023

www.doceblantpublishing.com

Cover by Fiona Jayde Media
Interior design by The Deliberate Page

Paperback ISBN: 978-1-7344646-6-5
Hardbound ISBN: 978-1-7344646-7-2
ePub ISBN: 978-1-7344646-8-9

Library of Congress Control Number: 2020939874

Printed in the United States of America
www.doceblant.com

Introduction

I had a lot of choices of different ideas for my fifth book, and as I was talking out loud and thinking about these one morning, I bounced this idea off my stepdaughter. So taking her guidance, I decided to write this very unique book about habits...aka rituals.

For those of you that read my *More What Color is Your Dog?* book, which was my third book, in chapter nine I get into *uncontrolled training environments (also called uncontrolled environments)*. In those kinds of environments you are not training your dog. Good examples of the behaviors that manifest in these environments are behaviors like resource guarding, aggression, barking, jumping, pulling on leashes, counter surfing, and digging. If your dog is allowed to play out these actions, and complete them, the behavior itself can be very reinforcing to him. So in essence, in an uncontrolled environment *the completion of the action is a reward*. The dog gets a payoff!

If a dog is allowed to playout any of these actions over a period of time, those same actions can become even more reinforcing to the animal. If allowed to escalate even more, they can intensify into some serious behavioral problems. Over time, these actions, that your dog that might have started at one point as just something very minimal, can escalate and become a pattern, habit or *ritual*. Once that happens it makes the behavior more difficult to get rid of, and that's why there are dog trainers.

Rituals are behavior patterns your dog might do on a daily basis and might only happen on occasions where there is a trigger involved. A trigger means there is a precursor to the behavior, and it is most often brought on by a person, place or thing. Rituals that your dog might develop can be something cute and funny, but they can also develop into something serious like aggression.

There are some great outcomes that can manifest from dogs developing rituals, as well. When rituals are built from a dog's natural personality that's based on a certain breed or mix of a dog, the results can actually be quite amazing! You'll read about this in chapter 4, The Game.

How about you? Do you have rituals that you act out around your dog? Owners can develop rituals as well, and sometimes these rituals can become precursors or triggers to rituals your dog might develop.

After training dogs for nearly five decades, as you might have guessed, I've seen a lot when it comes to animal behavior and bad habits that both dogs and people can develop. As a Hollywood dog trainer doing personal appearances, as well as teaching my dog trainer certification courses, I have gotten into the habit of watching the way people act around dogs. I have seen some very interesting things.

Of course, I could not go without adding some dog training to this book. So, in the last chapter, I am going to show you how to deal with some of the most common problem-solving issues and redirect your dog away from some bad behaviors before they actually become rituals.

I want to remind you that this book is really about you and your dog. I talked about this in my very first dog training video called *The Hollywood Dog Training Program* that was filmed in 1990. Back then, I said that the thing that makes dog training so amazing is that training your dog is based on two things: It is centered solely on the combination of you and your dog's personalities. That is what makes this relationship you have with your dog so special and unique.

Become your dog's best friend, love him, and respect him for who he is, because that chapter of your life will only last for about 15 years, sometimes less, and boy does it go by fast! Enjoy!

Table of Contents

CHAPTER 1

What is a Ritual?

If you define the word ritual (adj.), you will find the definition as, *"…an action when it is done in exactly the same way whenever a particular situation occurs that has to do with something a person does because it makes them feel good."* Let's separate that into three parts.

If you look at the beginning, it starts off *as an action when done in exactly the same way.* In the dog training world, you can translate that to "a behavior or action a dog performs that is played out the same way."

- The next part starts off with a very important word which is *whenever a particular situation occurs.* Whenever means that the "behavior or action" will not take place unless something happens. Unless what? Unless a particular situation occurs. In the dog training world, this is another name for a trigger, which can be defined as a "precursor to a behavior or action an animal plays out."

- And those few words are finally followed by *that has to do with something a person does because it makes them feel good.* This can be translated in the animal behavior world as "that has to do with something an animal does because it makes him feel good."

So to translate the whole definition of *ritual* (adj.) in the animal behavior world, it can be translated as *a behavior that makes the dog feel good which is played out the same way, only whenever a particular trigger occurs.* That makes a lot of sense!

Rituals are simply habits that are played out over and over, and you will learn that rituals do not happen overnight. They actually start off as a response to a stimulus, and as the dog gets the opportunity to play out that response or action, it simply makes him feel good.

If you take a look at an action your dog chooses to play out on his own, one of the reasons he takes it upon himself to play out that action is because it is so reinforcing to

Figure 1

him. It's his choice, and he knows better than anyone what he truly likes. A good example might be a dog that has a high prey drive that is gnawing on a Nylabone. If you look at a dog with a high prey drive, you can see by his actions there is no question he is 100% involved and excited about his toy. As a matter of fact, some dogs go crazy gnawing on a toy like that.

But I have found there is a huge difference between rituals your dog might play out naturally, like chewing on toys, and rituals that can be exhibited when you are training him.

Behavior patterns often become rituals over time. Whether a dog's response to something manifested from a particular thing that happened naturally or stemmed from something that occurred when you were training him, YOU have the ability to change your dog's natural character or makeup at that time.

The great thing about owning and working with dogs is that dog owners have different needs and priorities, and everyone has different things they want from their dog. There are times when you might want to build on a behavior pattern, and there might be times when you might want to eliminate a behavior pattern. When you build on a behavior pattern, and it escalates, you can create or build on a ritual of "drive." When you eliminate a behavior pattern from happening, you no longer give it a chance to build, meaning that an unwanted behavior pattern will stop. No ritual is created.

Whether a person wants to build on a behavior pattern and create a ritual of drive, or that person has a desire to get rid of a behavior pattern, it can be accomplished five different ways.

- **REDIRECTION** - The first way is to not allow the behavior pattern to become a ritual. The way this is accomplished is by redirecting your dog away from the behavior or habit he has developed. The most common way this is accomplished is by using a treat or even a high-value treat. This can work great in situations where the trainer is dealing with a dog that has a fear of people, places or things. It can also help with circumstances involving anxiety.

- **BUILDING ON DRIVE** - The second way is to build on the natural behavior the dog is showing you. This behavior can either be something that is triggered or something that came completely natural to the dog. The way this is accomplished is by channeling and building on the behavior that has developed. This is developed by increasing the energy level and drive, and by increasing a high level of play with an object or toy. This works excellently with working dogs as well as agility and flyball dogs.

- **TREATS AND MOTIVATION** - The third way is to teach the dog using something the dog really likes to eat. This is actually one of the most popular methods, as you are simply redirecting the dog by using a treat to train a behavior. It is almost always used in the teaching of most basic, intermediate, and advanced behaviors.

- **INTERRUPTING** - The fourth way is to not allow the action to play out. Remember that the completion of the behavior is reinforcing to the dog. By interrupting the behavior, you are stopping the action, and not allowing the behavior to play out. Over the course of the time, you will eventually extinguish the behavior. This is accomplished by using training tools for eliminating these unwanted behaviors.

- **SANCTUARY TRAINING** – The last way is called sanctuary training. Sanctuary training goes hand in hand in using redirection when you are dealing with fear. With sanctuary training, you are removing the person, place, or thing from the animal's presence, and by doing so, that is reinforcing to the animal.

So now let's briefly talk about these four methods.

Redirection – Redirection can work excellently when an owner or trainer has a dog that has developed some sort of fear of people, places, or things. The behavior might even be more severe, and the dog may also have developed some type of separation anxiety. With this particular training method, the owner or trainer uses a high-valued treat to redirect the dog. By using something that's motivating and redirecting, the dog now changes his focus away from the thing that is causing the fear and now focuses on the owner or trainer.

If the treat you are working with is greater than the fear of the person, place or thing, then redirection can be a great method. The problem I have seen with some owners and trainers that have tried to use this method in the past, is they did not find a treat that was more interesting to the dog than what he was afraid of.

That is why trainers use a very important term which is *high-valued treat* when talking about redirection. High-valued treat is an excellent name, and really describes what it is. It is a treat that is given to the dog ONLY in certain situations and is something that the dog sees as greater than the fear of the person, place or thing. We will be talking about training using redirection in the last chapter of the book.

Building and Channeling - The method of building drive and channeling energy are about as different from using redirections as can be possible. When we are building and channeling, and we have found something the dog goes crazy over to use as a reward, we are building on that. There are a variety of things dogs can naturally go crazy over, but most of the time they are squeaky toys, soft toys, tug toys, and balls.

When you are teaching a dog with high prey drive and the animal is naturally reactive, it is amazing how this style of training can be extremely successful for you. This is why this method is used so much with dogs that are trained for narcotics and explosive detection. Police and military also use this form of training for bite work as well, and I know a number of top flyball and agility trainers that use the routine too.

By building drive, channeling energy, and using things that can elevate your dog's personality and drive, you now have the ability to motivate and bring out that natural behavior even more. This creates a wanted ritual.

Interruptions - We also might want to go in a totally opposite direction from building drive, and the way we do this is by decreasing the reactiveness and eliminating the ritual, such as growling, biting, resource guarding, pacing, jumping, and so forth. The list goes on and on. If you want to decrease the drive, you would do it by interrupting the behavior. This is accomplished by using some kind of training tool, and interruptions are really the only ways to eliminate some of these behaviors in most dogs. There are some trainers that will try to redirect a dog using a high-value treat to get rid of these

behaviors. In most cases redirection will not work because once the dog is in that mode of prey drive, it is very difficult to get him out of it.

Let's imagine a Jack Russell Terrier killed a rabbit last night in the backyard, and there is

Figure 2

another rabbit in the backyard today. You have two options in dealing with this issue: they are to use either redirection or interruptions. In using redirections, the high-value treat has got to be greater than what you are redirecting your dog away from. Judging by the breed of dog (being a Jack Russell Terrier), and the fact that he killed something recently, the dog's desire and drive to want to kill the rabbit is most likely going to be greater than that of the high-value treat, or anything you have. In short, there is nothing you have that will be greater than the dog's desire to go after the rabbit. We will talk about the training, and interruptions in more detail later on in the book.

Figure 3 – On the set of A GOOD YEAR, 2005, Bonnieux, France

Treats and Motivation – It always blows me away when I hear dog trainers make blankets statements like, "you should never use treats to train your dog." If you are using treats to train a behavior, and never have any plans to fade out the treat, that is a problem. But using treats to train behaviors by using positive reinforcement, in most cases, is one of the most important aspects of dog training. The reason for this is that you are motivating the animal. As a Hollywood dog trainer for decades, I can personally tell you there is no way any of the trainers that worked on any of the TV shows, films, and commercials would have been able to train what they trained in the short amount of time they had, without the use of treats and motivation.

The use of treats as motivation are used just as much in the training of basic behaviors as they are in the training of advanced behaviors. The most amazing thing is that a ritual is created, where the dog gets excited over the fact he is going to get treats in his training sessions! The animal becoming predictable as you are getting ready to train him, getting excited prior to the session, and in his head knowing what is going to be happening, is what it is all about. Once the training session starts, you now have a dog that is ready to go!

Sanctuary Training – This is a style that I learned years ago. And believe it or not, the way I learned how to use it was not with dogs. This is a great style for the training of birds that have a fear of people. We will talk more about this in the chapter on fear and excitement, but I actually used it extensively in the training of penguins, pigeons, and seagulls.

Your Dog

If you look at your dog's natural personality, you'll see that your dog is totally different from any other dog. I talk a lot about your dog's natural personality as a speaker, in my previous books, DVDs, TV series, and dog trainer certification courses. The reason I am so passionate about this is because in order for you to train your dog, you really need to take a good look at the personality and teach the dog based on that individual persona. This is not a secret. I have had the chance to meet some of the best dog trainers in America as I have spoken at national dog training conferences, and almost every one of them carries that same philosophy!

You'll see the word *trigger* a lot in this book. It's a word I use often when teaching my dog trainer certification courses.

It is a word that animal trainers use that simply means something becomes precursor (trigger) to a behavior happening. This trigger *is* what initiates the behavior. A great example is your dog getting excited over food. There are some smaller dogs that spin around in circles when you are getting ready to put their dog bowl down to feed them. Your action of picking up the bowl frequently becomes a trigger. Another might be the vacuum cleaner that may get a dog excited or even scared. There are many other triggers that will be discussed later in the book.

The next chapter is going to focus on basic animal behavior. I am guessing many of you read my previous *What Color is Your Dog?* books, but I totally understand there are some readers that have not. The next chapter really gets into *What Color is Your Dog?* and personality-based dog training. It also will get into some habits, and even some common mistakes I have seen a number of dog owners and dog trainers develop. Some of these can actually be triggers and precursors to bad behaviors your dog might be playing out. We will also go into some of these later in the book.

Figure 4 - Speaking at the 2019 IACP Conference

In writing this book, chapter four was my favorite chapter to write and it's called "The Game". I believe it will really help you get inside your dog's head and understand the way he thinks. It will not only help you understand him, but also help you find ways to motivate him. Motivation is everything in training your dog.

The chapter will also help you to do the opposite, and instead of motivating, will help you eliminate some of the behaviors you do not want your dog to have the opportunity to play out.

Chapter four will also highlight working dogs, and dogs that are trained for narcotic and explosive detection, and bite work. And in the last part of chapter four, I will talk about some of the techniques that trainers or flyball and agility dogs use, and how that kind of motivation plays such a big part of dog training.

The last chapter of the book will help you deal with some bad habits your dog might have developed and will hopefully help you eliminate some of these problems before they become rituals. I am going to show you some great techniques to help you deal with some of the most common behavior problems like fear and excitement.

Extreme & Dangerous Rituals

Anyone who has met me will tell you I am probably one of the most optimistic people, so it gave me no joy to write this portion of the book. As a trainer for nearly five decades, I know that every dog owner has the right to know and understand about some very important things regarding animal behavior that are not the most enjoyable things to talk about.

Are some rituals untrainable? Unfortunately, yes. Are there some trainers that will have no success eliminating some serious aggression issues? Yes. Is it because they are not good trainers? No. It is because no one could have eliminated the problem. It was because the dog's response was something that had become an immediate response, and many of these serious aggressive responses could inflict serious injury and sometimes death to an animal or person.

The action, which is most often aggressive, might have been something that became a pattern or ritual. But it also may have become something more mental that was just a sheer response that bypassed all rationality. Quite often, in both of these scenarios, I would highly recommend getting an opinion from a veterinarian after you have explored all avenues of training.

There are some people that would want you to believe that you can train out every bad behavior from every dog. This kind of statement is incredibly irrational since the people making these statements are not living with the dog in question. Nor are they experiencing the safety and aggression issues of the people and animals that are exposed to the dog.

As I mentioned, there are some issues that might have started to escalate and increase over time. There are also some issues that have become a sheer response. When I talk about a sheer response, I mean it was something that bypassed all rationality, and the dog taking that very important second to think about things. Most dogs will take the time to do that. Instead of the dog taking the time to think, he did not and just reacted. This kind of response can be an extremely dangerous situation for people and animals around the animal. In some rare cases, like people, I am sure there are dogs that are born with brain disorders, or things that might change over time within his brain. Those are things veterinarians can help you understand.

This is why I highly recommend asking questions when you are dealing with serious aggression problems that might be in question. In these cases, you always want to seek a specialist, professional, as well as a veterinarian. By speaking to multiple veterinarians, it can help you make decisions with these serious issues that involve anxiety and aggression, that other trainers have had no success eliminating.

Natural Rituals

When I first decided to write this book, the one thing I thought that might be interesting was the opportunity to share with you some of the natural rituals that dogs perform. The behaviors I am talking about are behaviors patterns which happen naturally without the help of a human being. By dogs performing these behaviors over and over again, without the need of a human, over the course of time the behaviors can most likely become the dog's own unique rituals.

Throughout this book, and especially chapter three, I am going to be talking about understanding your dog's natural actions. The most important thing to understand in talking about natural rituals is that, in most cases, the dog is simply playing out a natural action of an ancestor: a wild dog, wolf, or possibly a coyote.

A good example of one of these actions is your dog walking in circles before he goes to sleep. If you watch a dog before he goes to sleep, your dog will have a ritual that he has developed over time. Your dog probably looks different and does something different than other dogs.

Most dogs will walk in circles before they go to sleep, and sometimes they can be very tight circles. With some dogs, the circle is so tight, that they literally pivot their back feet, so they rotate in the same spot. Some dogs will even do a large number of revolutions. Some dogs will combine the tight circles with nudging of the area with their nose and some dogs will begin to dig at the area. If the area they are sleeping on consists of blankets or something they can move, they might even spend a lot of time nudging, digging, and creating a kind of nest for themselves.

I have always been entertained by watching my own dogs create their own unique ritual before they go to sleep for the evening. I wondered what was going through their heads at the time of the particular behavior. What made them do the behavior?

If you listen to what a number of animal behaviorists believe, it is thought that back when dogs were wild, they needed to create and build a bed when they wanted to sleep. You can imagine that there was probably a safe area that was somewhere off the beaten path. The area was most likely made of sticks, rocks, and grass that the animal had found to sleep in. In order to create the bed or a nest, the dog would most likely have needed to start moving things in order to create a more comfortable area. If there were sticks or rocks in that area, there were only a few ways the dog could have moved them, and that was by either nudging them with their nose, grabbing them with his teeth and moving them, or digging and moving them with their front paws. Once the sticks or rocks were moved, the dog might have had the desire to knock down the grass and create more of a flattened area. The dog moving around in tight circles over the grass would have probably caused the grass to flatten out.

So, the next time you are going to go to sleep, check out your dog's ritual before he goes to sleep. And because that happens every day, at pretty much the same time, it is truly a ritual.

If your dog does something that is interesting and funny, without your help, email me at joel@joelsilverman.net. We might create another book based on YOUR dog's natural rituals!

CHAPTER 2

Animal Behavior

I want to start off with talking about animal behavior in general for a number of reasons, and the biggest one comes from some of the things I have learned in the past few years. In January 2017, I launched my Joel Silverman's Dog Trainer Certification Courses and as I write this book, we have now certified over 200 trainers with all three of our JSDT1, JSDT2, and JSDT3 classes. In these past three years, I have had the opportunity to meet a lot of people, and it verified what I thought for a long time. That is, that although almost all new pet owners and new professional dog trainers love their dogs, want to train them, and have good intentions, they often need direction. If new pet owners or new trainers do not get direction early on, they can develop bad habits, and those habits can frequently lead to bad training sessions. A great way to eliminate the chance of developing bad habits is to make sure a few things happen in the very beginning of training.

First, make sure you are aware of your actions, and these actions have to do with the way you walk, talk, move, reward, and correct. Remember that all dogs are different, and the actions you play out are going to vary greatly from dog to dog. There are little things you can do to either help or hinder your dog training sessions with regard to those actions.

The second part starts off with understanding that there is always a foundation that is a part of every behavior in dog training. The basic behaviors I am talking about are sit, stay, come, lie down, place, and heel. The foundation is exactly what the name says, and that is the basis of the behavior. If the foundation is strong, the behavior is going to be strong. If the foundation is weak and lacking, the behavior is going to be weak. How do you create a strong foundation? This is accomplished by taking your time and spending a lot of time on those early stages of the behavior, and those early stages are what make up the foundation. If you move too fast, and not enough time is spent on those early stages, the foundation is going to be weak.

Bad Habits

The most successful dog trainers I have met are the ones that have not developed bad habits. But I will also tell you I have seen some dog trainers that have been training dogs for 20 years, that developed a number of bad habits. Just because you've been training dogs for 20 years does not necessarily mean you are a good dog trainer. Bad habits that you have developed, without knowing it over the course of time, can become human habits or rituals. If you are someone who teaches others, and you have bad habits, more than likely, those bad habits will be passed on to either your clients or new dog trainers that you are teaching.

Some of the habits I will talk about are actions that some of you might unknowingly be doing right now, and much of these have to do with how you might move, stand, walk, talk, reward, or correct. These facets, along with the tools you use, can either help or hinder the training of your dog. This is why making the right choices is really what dog training is all about, and those alternatives are based solely on the individual dog you are training, at that specific time, and at that specific place.

What Color is Your Dog?®

We are going to start off talking about personality-based dog training, and my What Color is Your Dog?® training style. Then, later on in the chapter, I want to talk about some things to remember when training your dog. We will also get into some of the common bad habits I believe a lot of new pet owners develop, which can turn into unwanted rituals in their dog training sessions.

There have always been two simple points to my method of dog training:

The first part is understanding that the most important thing you can do is simply become your dog's best friend. This starts off with building an awesome relationship that's built on trust and love. It really is like putting fuel in a gas tank, because if there is no fuel in the tank, the car is not going anywhere. Without the relationship and bond, you are never going to be able to get your dog to be the best he can be, and the same thing can be said for your training sessions. When you develop a relationship, you get your dog to a place where he wants to please you and make you happy. The great news about building relationships is that it lays a great foundation for dog training. When your dog wants to please you and make you happy, training is going to be a lot easier, and that is something no dog trainer can argue with.

There are actually three steps involved in this process of bond building, and the whole process can last from as little as three days, to as much as a few weeks.

1. The first step is *to get to know your dog*. Take a few days to learn about the things your dog likes, and the things your dog does not like. You are not necessarily incorporating those things; you are just learning.

2. The next phase involves *developing a relationship*. This is accomplished over the next few days by incorporating all the things your dog likes and eliminating the things your dog does not like. If you do this over the next week, you have done everything to enhance your relationship and nothing to jeopardize your relationship.

3. Once this is accomplished, the last phase is *creating the bond* where you just are building a more solid relationship and trust. Once this bond is created, your dog will really want to please you, and you are now ready to start training your dog. Remember, when your dog wants to please you, training is going to be much easier. If there is one thing almost all dog trainers can agree on, the bond and relationship is everything.

Getting to know your dog is where it all starts! The last step is *creating the bond*, but you cannot possibly *create the bond* unless you complete the phase before that, which is *developing a relationship*. And you cannot *develop a relationship* unless you complete the phase before that which is *getting to know your dog*. So the bottom line is dog training all begins with *getting to know your dog*, and training your dog based on what your dog needs and wants.

This leads to the second part of my system, which is not really a style or method of dog training at all. It involves what I call personality-based dog training. That simply means that we want to train each dog based on his personality or character. I think a mistake that new pet owners and new dog trainers make is thinking that a dog's personality will stay the same. That could not be further from the truth. The reality is, your dog's personality will change over time, and your dog's personality can even change within seconds during a training session when you add or remove a variety of stimuli.

I really believe that whether you learn how to train dogs from me, or other trainers, personality-based dog training is and will be the future of dog training. It is essential you understand that all dogs, like people, all have their own personalities. Over my long career, the best dog trainers I have ever met were the ones that could take a look at the dog, get to know the dog, develop a relationship, and train the dog based on that unique personality, understanding the dog's personality can also change.

In the mid 2000s, as I started to try to find ways to make training easier for the public, I tried to find ideas that were easy to comprehend and easy to duplicate. I also did this for humane societies and animal shelters, so that when someone adopted a dog, they had an idea of what kind of training, and how much of it the dog would need.

What I did was create a color spectrum, which is pictured below, and made it with five colors of dogs.

To make it easy to understand, the closer your dog is to the center of the color spectrum, the easier it is to train. The farther away it is from the center of the color spectrum, the more challenging training will be. I did this for a number of reasons, but the most important reason was for pet owners that just adopted a dog. I think that it is essential when a person adopts a dog, he gets an honest understanding of what is in store for him, in the future, with the dog he wants to adopt. If training is going to be a little more challenging, he deserves to know that from the very onset.

I really believe a lot of dogs are returned to animal shelters because the owners adopted a dog that was more of a challenge than anticipated. Sometimes new pet owners might be given the impression that the new dog is going be easier to train than it really will be. When someone is given that overly optimistic feedback on training from the start, but the adopted dog is more challenging, it is easy for some people to simply just *give up*. But if owners have a rational idea of what is in store from the very beginning, it gives them a chance to comprehend and understand what they need to do before they adopt the dog. Once they have this information, they then can make a sensible decision, and make sure that the dog is the right dog for them prior to adopting.

What you are going to find is that your dog is actually one of nine colors. One of the mistakes I made in my first book, *What Color is Your Dog?* was to only focus on the five colors, but the truth is there really are nine. That is one of the reasons I wrote the follow up book, *More What Color is Your Dog?* So, in this chapter, we are going to show you that there is really a total of nine colors.

So let's look at the first five colors. Starting off in the center, we have the yellow dog in the middle.

The closer the dog is to the center of the spectrum, the easier it is to train. The farther the dog is away from the center, the more challenging it will be to train.

As you can see, we have the yellow dog in the middle, and that is because this dog will be the easiest to train. So what makes a dog yellow? Some dogs are either naturally yellow, meaning that they were simply mellow yellow their entire life. But some dogs might have been either green or orange and became yellow, mellowing over the course of time. You will see in a few minutes that your dog can change colors.

Let's start off with the cooler colored dogs. You can see that next to the yellow dog to the right is a green dog, which is the first of our cooler colored dogs.

Green dogs are naturally timid, shy, or apprehensive. About 30-35% of dogs in animal shelters and humane societies are, in fact, green dogs. You can see as we move farther away from the center, to the right of the green dog, we have the blue dog.

Blue dogs are extremely afraid of a variety of people and things. These are the dogs you might see run away from you or hide under the bed when you walk into someone's house. Only about 1–3% of dogs in animal shelters or humane societies are blue dogs. The blue and green dogs are what we call cooler colored dogs because of the cool colors.

On the other side of the yellow dog we have the warmer colored dogs.

If you look to the left of the yellow dog, we have the orange dog. Orange dogs are on the high-strung side with a lot of energy, meaning they are going to want to pull on the leash, pace, and jump on people, or possibly even bark excitedly. About 30-35% of dogs in animal shelters and humane societies are orange dogs. To the left of the orange dog, we have the red dog at the end of the color spectrum. Red dogs are even more high strung than the orange dog, as the energy levels of those behaviors I just mentioned are even more elevated. They are going to want to pull more, jump on people more, and bark more. Only about 2–5% of dogs in animal shelters and humane societies are red dogs.

Reds and oranges are the warmer colored dogs. These are dogs that will be more high-strung because they are more *reactive*. A reactive dog is pretty much as the name describes. Reactive dogs, or dogs with a high prey drive, simply react to people, places, and things more than other dogs. There are stimuli that are introduced, which will also increase the energy level of red or orange dogs. We'll talk more about reactive dogs more extensively in the book.

Blues and greens are the cooler colored dogs. These are dogs that will be less *reactive*. At the same time, because of their caution or apprehension, there are some things we might introduce that can escalate this behavior and make that anxiety or fear worse. So, just like the orange dog becoming more reactive and developing into a red dog, the green dog can become more timid and shy, and develop into blue.

Because of their energy level and reactiveness, the techniques involved in training *warmer colored dogs* are going to involve aspects where you need to have more control. All of these mannerisms will involve the way you walk, talk, move, reward, and correct or interrupt a behavior.

Because of their apprehensiveness, the techniques involved in training *cooler colored dogs* do not involve methods in which you need to have more control, because you simply don't need it. Instead, it involves motivation on your part to bring *out* the dog's personality. As with teaching the warmer colored dogs, this will be accomplished by the way you walk, talk, move, reward, and correct or interrupt a behavior.

Assessing Your Dog's Color

Now that you have an idea of the color spectrum, you can get a good picture of your dog's color. But there is a catch: Remember that dog training is fluid and is constantly changing. As a dog is being trained and is learning, quite often the color will change, and the dog will always move toward the center of the color spectrum. A red can become orange, and orange can become yellow. The same thing applies to the cooler colored dogs. A blue dog can become green, and a green dog can become yellow. Will a red Jack Russell Terrier ever be a yellow dog? Probably not, but he can become an orange dog.

The first question you might ask is, "Can my dog be different colors?" The answer to that is yes. Dogs can change colors, sometimes even within a few minutes. Although your dog might be a timid green dog naturally, there might be times when a stimulus can get excite him and get him to become reactive and turn into an orange dog.

A great example is you might have a green Labrador retriever that is naturally timid and shy in most situations. But when you take the dog in the front yard, and he sees other dogs, he gets excited and turns into an orange dog. Let's say that you are going to train your Labrador to heel in the front yard with those same distractions. Even though your dog is a natural green dog, the question is, when you are training your dog, what color is your dog in that actual training environment? If your green dog becomes reactive in the front yard around other dogs or things that excite him in that environment, you are now training an orange dog. If you move the dog back in the house, and he mellows out and becomes a green dog, train him in the house as a green dog. Remember that the thing that makes dog training so fun and interesting is that it is constantly changing.

You'll learn more about this later in the book, but it's important to remember that your dog can change colors over time, as mentioned earlier. As your dog begins to calm down, a red dog can mellow and become an orange dog. The same thing applies to the orange dog; as he mellows out, he can become a yellow dog. If you look at the cooler colored dogs, the same applies. As your blue dog begins to become less timid and afraid, a blue dog can become a green dog. The same applies with the green dog; as he becomes less timid, he can become a yellow dog. Remember, as your dog begins to learn and understand, he will always move to the center of the spectrum.

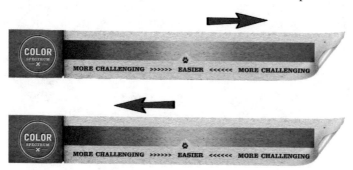

I mentioned that there are actually nine colors of dogs. As your dog begins to change colors, you will notice that he might start off green. But as you socialize him and begin training him, he becomes a green/yellow. The reason for this is because he is not timid, but not quite yet a mellow yellow dog. He might stay like that for a while before he actually becomes yellow. If you are starting off with a blue dog that is extremely afraid of things, as you socialize him, he may very well become blue/green, and he might stay like that for a while. Over the course of time, he might become green.

The same thing applies to the warmer colored dogs. Your dog might start off as an orange dog, but as you start to socialize him and calm him down and begin training him, he becomes orange/yellow. The reason for that is he is not quite a yellow dog yet, but not an orange dog. He might stay like that for a while before he actually becomes yellow. If you are starting with a red dog that is overly reactive of things, as you socialize him, he may very well become red/orange, and he might stay like that for a while. Over the course of time, he might become orange.

So, here are the nine colors:

Red – Red/Orange – Orange – Orange/Yellow – Yellow – Green/Yellow – Green – Blue/Green - Blue

The Foundation

I want to start with this element of dog training because I think it so often gets overlooked. You will hear me talk about this a number of times in this book, but *the foundation is everything* when it comes to dog training.

Just like a structure, if the foundation is weak, the structure will break. Dog training is no different. Every complete behavior is nothing more than a series of small steps, and the early steps are the most important ones. If an owner or trainer is training a dog and moving through the steps too fast, and not focusing on those early steps, even though the behavior is trained, the dog will most likely not have a strong behavior. The reason is because the owner or trainer did not spend enough time working on those early phases, so the foundation is going to be weak.

Dogs can actually give you a false sense of security when a behavior *you think* is trained. They can be doing exactly what you asked, but not truly understanding what they are doing. You want to make sure when you ask your dog to do a behavior, that the dog not only performs the behavior but, most importantly, understands what he is actually doing. It all starts with taking your time, spending more time on the early steps, and building that foundation.

I am going to give you the same example that I talk about in my dog trainer certification courses. We will talk about the "stay" behavior a little later in this chapter, but I like to use this particular behavior as a good example of how I focus on the foundation and spend a lot of time on those early steps.

I always like to use the example of starting to teach a brand-new dog to stay on a Monday, and the goal would be to have the dog staying on camera for a shot from 20 feet away that following Friday. So, in essence, I would have four days to teach this behavior. If you saw a number of dog trainers or owners, they would most likely focus on some control the first half of the day and step back to three to four feet by the end of the first day. The next day they might move a few more feet back, and that would take place every day until they got 20 feet away. That sounds about right to most people. However, the issue I have with that approach is that the foundation was never laid because the trainer never spent enough time on those early phases. Even though I am only spending four days to teach the dog, I still understand that I need to build that foundation and control.

The difference with me is that I understand when teaching the stay behavior, there are two variables, and those are time and distance. Time is how long the dog is staying, and distance is how far away we get from the dog. The majority of dog trainers and dog owners try to train both of those aspects at the same time, and I do not.

I believe that the best way to build the foundation for that particular behavior is to stand next to the dog and do nothing more than build up the amount of time the dog is staying. So, I would stand right next to the dog and focus on time and control, not distance. If I am right next to the dog, each time he breaks from that position (and it is going to happen), I am there to interrupt that behavior right away and get the dog back in a sitting position. Timing is everything in dog training. You cannot do what I just did from four feet away because that interruption has to happen when you are right next to the dog. But if you can spend a whole day or two doing what I just did, and create the dog sitting and staying for 30-45 seconds, and watching you, you have now built an incredible foundation in that short period of time.

When you have that type of control, quite often you can start stepping back three to four feet at a time. The reason you can do that is the dog has now built a solid foundation. Remember that those first few days he has already been interrupted dozens of times and understands that if he gets up from that position, you are just going to get him back into that same position. He gets rewarded for that.

The trainer who starts moving way too fast and begins stepping back four feet at the end of the first day is most likely going to have problems because he did not spend enough time *letting the dog make that mistake*. Remember when you are teaching your dog to "stay," all dogs are going to break eventually from that position. Timing is everything, and you need to be there to interrupt the dog at that time. But if you are four to six feet away, your interruption is going to be way too late, *and saying "uh-uh" from six feet away is not going to cut it.*

By spending time on the early parts of all behaviors, you build a great foundation, and the dog begins to truly understand what he is doing.

Uh-Uh

Since I just mentioned the uh-uh thing, I want to talk about it. If this is something you need, or want to say from time to time, I totally understand, and if your dog is working well, by all means you should do that.

However, since I launched my certification courses, I have seen a number of people that have developed some really bad habits by using the word constantly. If you are going to use that word, I think it is fair to ask yourself what the word actually means. When I hear someone using "uh -uh" constantly, the first thing I ask them is, "what does that word mean?" No one can seem to tell me. Does it mean "no"? If you cannot tell someone what a word means that you are using to train your dog, how can you expect your dog to understand what it means.

More times than not, people use this word because the dog is getting ready to do something like break from a stay position or is getting ready to do something they do not want, and they say "uh-uh." If you are training your dog to stay, don't be afraid to let your dog fail. Instead of worrying about the dog breaking, let your dog break from that position but immediately interrupt and bring the dog back, and then repeat the behavior. This way you let the dog figure things out on his own. If you say "uh-uh," and never let your dog break from that position, he never gets a chance to make a mistake. This creates a lack of opportunity for the dog to learn what is right and wrong.

Mistakes

There is no doubt that dogs are going to make mistakes. Remember that your dog doing things incorrectly is all a part of learning. They will never learn how to do something right if they never do it wrong. Let your dog make mistakes because it is a huge part of the learning process.

Body Language

Your body language plays a big factor in the training of cooler and warmer colored dogs, and is made up of how you walk, talk, and move around your dog. One of the reasons I came up with the *What Color is Your Dog?* training method is because the training, including body language, differs so much between the warmer and cooler colored dogs.

With the cooler colored dogs, your actions may be a bit more animated to bring out the dog's personality. If you think about it from your dog's perspective: you tell your dog to "stay" from ten feet away and you start to move parallel to your dog with a bit of a faster pace, that movement will make the dog *want* to watch you. Because of your movement, it often creates interest from the dog's perspective, and that's what you want to build with cooler colored dogs. You want the cooler colored dogs to feel excitement with what you are doing.

On the other hand, if you are working with a warmer colored dog with a lot of energy, you are going to want to move in a way that controls the dog. If you were to use the same technique that you used with the cooler colored dog and you move parallel and a bit faster, because the animal is more reactive, it is highly likely the dog will want to break from that position to go to you.

So, instead of moving faster, when working with warmer colored dogs, you are going to want to slow yourself down and make all your movements more deliberate. As the warmer colored dog begins to get used to you moving around, you can start moving around a bit faster.

Your Voice

Your voice is another huge aspect of dog training, which I believe is so commonly overlooked. It can also change based on the color of the dog you are training. A number of pet owners forget that sometimes a voice correction can be just as detrimental to their dog as a physical correction.

Cooler Colored Dogs

With a number of cooler colored dogs adopted from animal shelters and humane societies, most of the time, we will not know their true history. If they come from an abusive past, and the previous owners have yelled and screamed at them, there is a good chance that simply raising your voice can result in the dog becoming scared. You can tell by just watching the way he responds: actions like holding the tail between his legs, standing in a slouched position, cowering, shaking, or wanting to run. You might also see some various forms of fear/aggression merely from you saying the word "no." This is really why I encourage all pet owners to get to know their dogs when they first adopt them. If you take the time and get to know your dog, you can catch many of these signs from the very beginning. Sometimes based on a horrible past or just saying a particular word like "no" can trigger some of these responses.

- The solution in retraining your cooler colored dog that might have these kinds of issues is to start by not yelling or raising your voice to your dog.

- If there is a word that triggers these responses, *eliminate* that word, and use a different word.

- If you no longer raise your voice, and eliminate words that can scare your dog, you not only give your blue dog a chance to go green, or your green dog a chance to go yellow, but also build a great trusting relationship between you and your dog.

Warmer Colored Dogs

With your voice, regarding warmer colored dogs, there really is a 180-degree difference in the training between them and cooler colored dogs. Even though there is a huge change, let me start by saying that I do not believe in yelling, screaming, or raising your voice to your dog, except in emergency situations. I do, however, believe in changing inflections in your voice based on the color of the dog you are working with.

One of the biggest mistakes new pet owners will make with warmer colored dogs, regarding their voice, is to ask a dog to do something instead of telling the dog. If you make it a *statement* and not a *question*, your dog can receive that statement and view you as emotionally taking charge. Anyone who has been to my classes or seminars will continuously hear me tell my students or audience, "make it a statement… not a question." Remember that dogs want to be told what to do. You tell them what to do, and when they complete the task, you let them know. Your appreciation is what the dog is truly working for.

Another mistake owners can make with warmer colored dogs is to keep the same tone of voice for everything. Even though the tone of your voice may be low most of the time, there are times you may need to increase the tone without yelling. One of the times this will happen is when you tell your dog to sit and stay as you add distractions. As you begin to add distractions, there might be times where you need to have more control by saying "stay" a bit louder. So when you are training warmer colored dogs, remember there are times when you are going to want to add inflections or increase the tone of your voice.

Your Dog's Neck Area

Before you train your dog, as you take the time to get to know your dog, one of the first things you will want to find out is if your dog is sensitive around his neck area. From the very beginning, you just need to be conscientious when putting any collar on any dog you do not know—this also includes flat collars. I would also be aware when you touch the collar or his neck as well. You don't want to be paranoid, but you want to see if your dog is a little hesitant when you get your hands around his neck area.

If your dog is sensitive around his neck area, there are a few reasons for that, all based on the past. There might be a chance that someone either grabbed the scruff of his neck or grabbed his collar. The person also might not have understood how to use a training collar correctly, or possibly over-corrected. I'll talk about training later in the book, but I will tell you there is *never* a reason to grab the scruff of your dog's neck. There is nothing that will increase the danger of the dog turning and biting someone more than constantly grabbing your dog's neck in that manner.

If, for some reason, your dog gets a little timid when you connect your leash to the collar, there is a good chance the dog was overcorrected or someone grabbed the scruff of his neck. Overcorrecting simply means someone has jerked on the leash very hard, and this is another action for which there is absolutely no excuse. As far as overcorrecting a dog is concerned, someone once said to me, "It's the fool… not the tool." Training tools are just that, and in the right situation and with the right dog, they can work excellently! The best trainers I have ever worked with understand this. This is accomplished by keeping any correction done with any training tool to a minimum.

Common Mistakes

Since I launched my dog trainer certification courses, I have seen and heard a lot of the same fallacies. So, I want to give you just a few tips that will hopefully put an end to some of those misconceptions.

- Training Sessions – Some people still believe that the longer time you spend training your dog, the smarter the dog will be. That could not be further from the truth. You want to train your dog with short two to three-minute training sessions, which will leave the dog wanting more. Over the course of time, you can start to increase the length of the training sessions. If you engage in long training sessions from the very beginning, make it boring, and burn the dog out, training is not going to be fun.

- Multiple Cues – To give *multiple cues* simply means you are giving your dog more than one cue to do a behavior. An example is telling your dog to "sit" more than one time. If you teach your dog to become conditioned to you giving multiple cues for the "sit" behavior, you are most likely going to have to always tell your dog to "sit" more than one time.

- Confidence – If you bring your dog out for a training session, and have no game plan for the session, or no confidence in what you are doing, smart dogs will read that body language. Have a goal of what you want to accomplish before you bring your dog out and send the message to your dog that you have confidence (even though you might not necessarily).

Breaking Behaviors Down

People that have gone through my dog trainer certification courses, or who have heard me speak at appearances and events, know that I break every behavior down into small steps before I teach the dog.

Remember that a behavior is nothing more than a series of small steps, so we focus on one step at a time. It is also important to understand that all dogs learn at different speeds, and some dogs might learn specific steps faster than others. A good example is comparing an intelligent Border Collie to an Afghan (nothing against Afghans). There is no question the Border Collie is going to learn much faster than the Afghan. Nonetheless, both dogs will be taught every stage of every behavior. When you break behaviors down, for example, the *sit* and *lie down* behaviors, each will have about six to seven steps.

Using the Border Collie as an example, you will start with the first step, move on to the second step, and so on. Because of the intelligence level, you might be at step four within about 45 seconds with that Border Collie, but the only reason is that you started with the first step. He understood and so you moved on to the second step, and so on.

But with other dogs, like the Afghan, you start with step one, and you might be on that step for a number of training sessions or maybe even a day or two. This is why it is essential to look at each dog as an individual, start with step one, and move on to the next step as the dog understands that step.

The Release

I think another mistake that new pet owners make, that just started teaching their dog new behaviors, is not actually releasing the dog when they are finished with training the behavior they are teaching. Remember that when you are training your dog, there are four things that are going to happen.

1 - The cue – The first is that you are going to give your dog a cue. This will be a visual or verbal cue. I teach both cues, and this *stimulus* is what starts everything.

2 - The response – Your dog will respond to your cue one way or another, so your dog will either be correct (right) or incorrect (wrong).

3 - Your response – If your dog is correct, you are going to reward the dog. If your dog is incorrect, you are going to interrupt the dog and repeat the process.

Most pet owners will end it right there, meaning they will reward the dog for being correct and walk away. The only problem is the dog released himself.

4 - The last phase is the release. What you want to do is release the dog after you reward him. My release consists of something both verbal and physical. I will say the word "Okay" very loud, and also pat the dog on his side. If you do not release the dog, *he will be releasing himself after he is rewarded*, and the dog can get into a pattern or ritual of releasing himself. Not a good ritual.

One last thing about the release. Many of the dogs you will train come from three main groups. They are the working, herding, and sporting groups. If you think about German Shepherds and mixes, Golden Retrievers and mixes, or Labrador Retrievers and mixes, that covers a large percentage of dogs. These dogs are bred to want to work and please.

By you giving the dog that affirmation and release, you are confirming that what they did was good, and most importantly, that they completed the task. That is dog training 101.

Cues - We are not going to talk much in this book about all the different cues I teach. However, for clarity, a cue is something that you give the dog to let the dog know what you want him to do. A great example is when you give the dog a cue which will tell him to sit, you will give him a totally different cue to tell him to lie down, and so on. I teach my clients and students two different cues for each behavior, and they are verbal and visual cues.

When your dog is trained, the way you know the dog understands the verbal or visual cue is to give the dog *only* one cue. Start with giving a verbal cue, and if the dog understands, then give the dog *only* the visual cue. You do this by giving just a verbal cue with no hand cues, keeping your hands to your side. If he completes the behavior you know he understands the verbal cue. Now do the same thing except just give the dog the visual cue without saying anything. If he completes the behavior, you know he understands the visual cue.

When giving your dog any cue, you want to make sure you are consistently giving him the same cue. I see a lot of breakdown of behavior with dogs, and most of the time it comes from people not being on the same page. It occurs when everyone in the house gives different cues, and once this happens, it can be very confusing for the dog. So make sure everyone is on board, and everyone gives the same cues.

The Training Session – It is essential that your dog wants to work. There are several things you can do to make the training sessions fun and something that the dog looks forward to, and chapter three will go into that. There are also a number of things you can do to make the training session a negative thing and something the dog does not look forward to.

One of the ways training becomes negative to the dog is when the pet owner puts the animal through long, drawn-out training sessions. The goal to training your dog is to make the training session a fun thing, and it is not going to be enjoyable if it is long and boring. So remember to keep your training sessions short, and only about two to three minutes in the very beginning. You also want to end every training session on a positive note and end the session with the dog always wanting more!

There is a lot to a training session, and my philosophy has always been to make the session as effective as possible.

- The training session starts off with planning, and the planning should always take place *before* the actual training session itself.

- When you plan the session, you want to have a goal of what you want to accomplish during the session.

- A mistake pet owners make is not having a goal of what they want to accomplish. Any doubt or uncertainty that you portray to your dog, is very easily picked up by your dog.

- Remember, by not having a goal, and just bringing your dog out to train, you run the risk of a few things. First of all, because you are not sure of what you want to do, your dog can very easily pick up on that lack of confidence. Secondly, if you do not have an understanding of what you want to train, you run the risk of creating a *marathon* dog training session. The results of this are often to burn out the dog in the very first session. By this happening, from the very beginning, the dog can perceive the training session as a negative thing.

The solution are these simple things:

- Plan out the training session before you bring the dog out.

- Break the behavior into small steps before you bring the dog out and have an idea of what step of the behavior you are going to work on.

- Have a goal of what you want to accomplish and keep the sessions between one to three minutes.

- If you are using a treat, make it something the dog really likes. To use something the dog could care less about is an absolute waste of you and your dog's time.

- When you bring the dog out, train the phase you want to teach three to four times, and then move onto something else. Just keep moving and make it fun.

- When you are finished with the session, use the release that we talked about earlier. This lets the dog know he completed the task, and you let him know what he did was great!

- Always end each training session on a positive note.

- When the training session is completed, spend time with the dog just petting, playing, or walking afterward. This makes the end of the session that much more reinforcing to the dog.

- Most importantly, you have now created a good pattern and ritual in regard to your dog training session.

Methods of Dog Training – As we talked about earlier in this chapter, I think there is a misconception among some new pet owners and some dog trainers thinking for some reason there is some "cookie cutter" way to train dogs. Take the time to get to know and understand your dog before training, and train your dog based on his personality he is giving you at the time you are teaching him. Remember that personalities and your dog's color can change right in the middle of a training session.

A great example is the training of a Jack Russell Terrier. Let's imagine your dog is a green dog and you are teaching him to sit and lie down inside your home. If that is the case, you are most likely using some kind of treat for motivation. But let's say during the same training session, you decide to teach the heel behavior in the front yard. The only problem is the dog killed a rabbit in the back yard yesterday, and there are a few rabbits in the front yard. Because he killed the rabbit, and there are rabbits in the front yard, there is a good possibility that this green dog (that was working for treats in the house just seconds ago) could become an orange dog once you take a few steps into the front yard. If that is the case, you will train him as an orange dog.

Remember that personalities can change at the blink of an eye if there is something that elicits a response on a regular basis. When I am teaching my dog trainer certification courses, I always use this example about the changing of personalities and colors. Remember that dog training is a fluid, constantly changing process. As it changes, rituals can develop that can work for you or work against you.

Your Voice & Body Language – We talked about your voice and your body language a little earlier. I want to remind you again how much of a part they both play in dog training. It is essential you keep your actions as natural as possible. When I say your actions as "being natural," I mean you want to stay as natural as possible in the way you walk, talk, and move when you are teaching your dog. If, when you are giving a verbal cue, your dog becomes conditioned to you always raising your voice or yelling at him to do a behavior, you have created a pattern. Your dog most likely only going to respond to your verbal cue when you raise your voice or yell, as a result. But, if from the very beginning of training, you were to give only verbal cues in your normal tone of voice, he would become conditioned to take that cue from you with that certain low pitch.

Your body movement also plays a big part in dog training. When you are training behaviors like the *stay*, and you step back and start to create distance, try to move in the same manner you naturally move. This means when you back up, take longer strides as you do so. The same thing applies to moving side to side when you are training the *stay* behavior. That means taking longer strides, because that is what most people do when they move side to side. A common habit some dog owners make is to take tiny steps, and because that is unnatural, that could trigger a red flag and get the dog to break from the sitting position. The reason is, this simply is not the way you normally move. We'll talk more at this in "The Human" chapter.

Your Bridge or Marker – I see a number of behavior issues start with the owner or trainer who uses a bridge or marker that simply will not work for the dog at the time.

Let's start by explaining what a "marker" is. A marker or "bridge" is something that you are going to say, a sound you might make, or possibly using the sound of a clicker. This sound is simply a way to communicate to the dog that what he did was correct at that exact time. These markers are essential in almost any kind of animal training, and timing is just

as important. One of the characteristics almost all excellent dog trainers have is fantastic timing.

A "bridge" is the same thing as a marker (just a different name). Back when I trained marine mammals in the 70's

Figure 5 - Sea World,1983, San Diego, CA

and 80's, it was essential that we were able to let the dolphin or killer whale know that what he did was correct. The way we accomplished this was by using a high-pitched dog whistle that the animal could hear. One of the reasons these came in handy was because, quite often, the animal would be nearly 50-75 feet away when we wanted to let him know he did something correct. We used this same kind of bridge with sea lions and otters, but instead of the whistle we used a clicker. In both of those scenarios, once the animal hears the sound the animal comes back to us. The sound does NOT necessarily mean that we are going to reward with food. It simply means that what they did was correct. The reason they call it a "bridge" is because a bridge is the amount of time between from when the animal hears the sound and the animal is rewarded. Sometimes when you are training dolphins and killer whales that amount of time can be as much as 15–20 seconds. But the animal has that 15–20 seconds to digest what has happened at that exact time and realize he did the behavior correctly. When the animal comes to us, we decide what kind of reward, or if any reward, will be given. I want to make it clear that the bridge or marker simply lets the animal know when he does something right. It does not necessarily mean the animal is going to get a reward. If anyone tells you that you should always give a reward after the sound of the bridge or marker, they do not understand the way this tool was meant to be used. I will talk about this more later on.

Since those days, clicker training was introduced to dog training. But there is a huge difference between dog training and marine mammal training. In marine mammal training we have no choice in markers, so we use things like whistles for cetaceans (whales and dolphins), and we use

Figure 6 - Sea World, 1983, San Diego, CA

clickers for pinnipeds (sea lions, otters, etc.).

In dog training, it seems that a number of former marine mammal trainers have introduced clickers to dog training. Although these tools work great with pinnipeds and otters, I have never been a fan of using clickers with dogs for a few reasons:

- First of all, it ties up one hand, as you normally click with one hand, and reward with the treat with the other hand.

- Second, if you are constantly clicking with one hand, and feeding with the other, where is the dog

43

watching? Naturally, he will most likely watch the hand that is clicking and move his eyes to the hand that is feeding. I want the dog to watch me, not my hands.

- Third, and this is the biggest reason, in most cases, the response from the dog when he hears that clicker often becomes too much of a response. When I teach a behavior, and I let the dog know he did something correct, the way he responds is very important. For me, when I use a clicker, there is way too much of a response coming from the dog. A good example is, with most dogs, they get very excited when they hear the sound of a clicker. But that is not necessarily the reaction that I am looking for. Most of the time when I train advanced behaviors like a retrieve or an eye cover for a movie or TV show, I want to be able to tell the dog what he did was correct with a sound, have the dog be rational, reward the dog, and stay in the position he is in. By the dog being rational, I can then repeat what I was doing. However, if I use the clicker, because of the dog's excitement, he is most likely to get excited and gets up from a sitting position. As a result, I constantly have to reset things.

So, what do I recommend? Instead of a clicker, I recommend using the word "good" (or any word you like) as a marker.

- For one thing, by using a word and not using a clicker, it frees up your hand.

- Another great thing about using a word as a marker is that when it comes from your mouth, the dog has a better chance to stay focused on your eyes and face, rather than your hands.

- Lastly, by using the word "good" (or any other word), you can control the tone of your voice, which you want to be very subtle. Because of this, you will almost always see less of a response from your dog than you would when using a clicker.

Now that I have told you about the markers, and using the word "good," let me tell you why I do not like to use ANY marker for the first few days of dog training. You have to remember that a number of dogs that will be trained will be adopted from animal shelters and humane societies. Most average pet owners who train their dogs will tell the dog to do something and when the dog does what they asked, they will say the word "good" as they are rewarding the dog. Here is the problem with that. Most dogs will release themselves naturally when the owner says, "good." Most people think they are using the word "good" to let the dog know he did something correct, and do not understand that they are also releasing the dog. Because of this, there are now dual meanings of the marker to the dog. The word "good" is not only marking the behavior but is also used as a release.

Earlier in this chapter, I talked about the release and told you it was essential to use a separate word for that release to let the dog know that he completed his task. I told you that I like to use the word, "Okay." I also gave the dog a nice pat on his side at the same time. By doing both of these things, there is no question that I made it very clear to the dog that I was releasing him.

Here is where I start to see some problems early on. If you are looking to get control of your dog right from the onset, and you are teaching an orange dog to sit and stay, and you say "good" in a high-pitched voice as you reward the dog, he is most likely going to break from that position as you say "good" or you reward him. But you never released him. You can now see how you can be setting yourself up for a lot of problems down the road.

You have to remember that most dogs have become conditioned to being both rewarded when they hear the word "good" and released at the same time. You want to make sure that there are two separate distinct words your dog understands. He needs to know what he did was correct but is not released. He also needs to know there is a separate word that you will use that lets him know he is released.

Here is the way you would either train a dog or retrain a dog to understand these principles. You are going to start off by adding another valuable word I love to use early on, and that is the word "stay." You will also remove the word "good" for now, and you are going to substitute it with the word "stay." When you train your dog to sit, for example:

- When he gets in that sitting position that you like, say "stay."

- Reward him.

- Say "stay" again.

- Then release him by saying, "Okay," and giving him a nice pat on the side.

You can see by doing these few things, and separating these words, you start off with a huge amount of control. This is one of the reasons professional dog trainers call the sit and stay behavior the "sit-stay." You do this because even though you are not necessarily teaching the stay behavior, you are conditioning your dog early on to hear the word "stay," and you reward that, as well.

Now, over time, as your dog begins to understand and you get some control, you can THEN start adding "good" or whatever word you would like to use as your marker. This method works excellently, especially for dogs that have been adopted or are not necessarily taught the correct way from the very beginning.

Rewards & Corrections

When a person is teaching a dog, it is critical she understands there are two important variables that always play a major factor in planning the training session. They are: rewards and corrections. As you can imagine, based on the color of your dog, these two elements can change dramatically depending on the personality of the dog you are training, as well as the environments they are in. I want to take some time to talk about these two key aspects.

Rewards are also called *reinforcements* in the animal behavior world. And if you want to get fancy, the planning of the rewards is called a *reinforcement schedule*. The main reason for something like this is so that everyone training the animal is on the same page and is consistent with the training, and with what they are using to reinforce the animal.

The great part about animal behavior is that, quite often, we have a choice of many different types of rewards to use. It all depends upon the kind of animal and the personality of that particular animal. A great example of this is back in the days when I trained dolphins, sea lions, and killer whales. There were only a few different types of rewards. The one reinforcement we used was fish, but we used four to five different types. We also varied the amount of fish we gave the animal when he did something correct. The other reward was a tactile reward, which simply means petting the animal. So as you can see from the way we rewarded marine mammals, we had the opportunity to vary the amount of fish we gave the animal, vary the kind of fish, and we also added tactile rewards. This gave us a lot of things to alternate.

Something I just mentioned was the word "varying" the amount of food. When it comes to understanding rewards, and putting it all into play, variation and rewards go hand in hand. By varying the reward with your dog, you keep things interesting, and most importantly, unpredictable.

So, let's talk about dogs and variation in rewards. One great thing about dogs is that they all are different, and so many of them like a variety of different things. Those things that they really like are what you will use as a reward, so, the more things they like, the more of those things you can use. A great example might be a Labrador Retriever that likes people, treats, and toys. If we break each one of these down, we can create some variation within those individual rewards themselves.

With treats, as you can imagine, there are a huge variety of treats to use when training your dog. I have always been a huge fan of Bil-Jac treats. You will find that there is a lot of variation just within that brand of treats. But let's say you want to add a high-value treat at times like chicken, cheese, or beef. And, of course, you also have the ability to vary the amount of these treats you feed each time the dog is rewarded. As you can see, there is a lot of variation when using treats.

Now let's talk about toys. As you know there are a lot of toys to choose from to use as a reward. A great example is if your dog likes tugging on a toy, you can use that as a reward, and if he likes tugging on a few different toys, you can vary the tugging toys. If your dog likes chasing balls, try using those as well, and you can vary the kinds of balls he chases, too. So within the toy world, there is a vast amount of variation, as well.

And, of course, there are tactile rewards that involve petting the dog.

So as you can see, just these three variables give you the opportunity to introduce a vast amount of variation when training the dog.

I like to use treats to train most dogs to learn behaviors. Once the behavior is trained, I slowly fade the treat out. At that time, I also start to condition the dog to take the tactile reward in conjunction with the treat. As I do so, I am literally training and conditioning the dog to accept the tactile reward as a reinforcement. But make sure you start to fade out the treat or toy after the behavior is completely trained using treats.

I need to mention one last thing on rewards, and this is for you folks that might have red or orange dogs that you are looking to calm the dog down during the training session. Tactile rewards can work great—just make sure when you pet him, you do so in a slow and relaxed way. A mistake that some people make that are using a tactile reward with these dogs is to pet the dog very rough and sometimes around his face. Remember when you are training red or orange dogs, they are most likely a little or very high strung, and they are going to play off of you. If you are very rough with the way you pet your dog, that might have a tendency to increase that already high level of energy.

Instead, I recommend kneeling down to find a place to pet the dog that has a relaxing effect on the dog and where the dog will accept that tactile reward. I have found that when training reactive dogs, I try to stay away from their head and face when using tactile rewards, as petting the dog in those areas can have a tendency to increase their energy level. Instead, I recommend finding a different place to pet your dog, and there are a lot of them. I have found a place that works well for this is the area right around his sternum area. You will find that as you pet the dog very slowly, it can have a very soothing effect on the dog.

Corrections

Corrections are the second important variable involved in dog training. Remember that you will not only need to reward your dog, but your dog also needs to understand when he is not correct. Corrections are essential because they are the best way to communicate to the dog that what he did was not correct.

A number of ill-informed dog trainers believe that a correction is something bad, and something physical—that could not be further from the truth. Remember that your dog needs to understand what was right or wrong from the very beginning of training. A correction is nothing more than an interruption, and that interruption can change based on the particular dog, and what the dog is being trained to do. Most interruptions and corrections are simply asking the dog to repeat what you just requested, and what he did incorrectly. An interruption is, in fact, considered a correction.

Elevated Areas

The last thing I want to talk about are elevated areas. Elevated areas are a defined place, and they can be a variety of natu-

ral things like a chair, bed, sofa, landing, stairs, or your entrance to your house. You can build something simple, like the one I use (pictured).

The great part about training dogs on an elevated

area is that it is a defined place. There are a number of reasons elevated areas are one of my favorite and essential training tools.

These are great to train dogs on because it is easier on your back. But the best thing I like about it is it does not give your dog the opportunity to start to cheat.

- When training dogs on flat ground, you give them a chance to cheat by doing things like scoot forward while sitting or take a few steps toward you before sitting.

- But using an elevated area on a behavior like the *stay* makes it much easier on the dog because if he can only come so far forward without jumping or falling off, it eliminates cheating.

- And the great part about it is if he jumps off the elevated area, he is just guided back up.

- Early on in teaching this behavior, by not "making" the dog stay and letting him make mistakes, over the course of time, he figures it out on his own. Just keep your actions as natural as possible. It starts off with standing straight and not hunched over. Also, keep your right hand back near your shoulder. And the last thing is, when you step back, take long strides the way you would normally back up.

- So make elevated areas a part of your training ritual!

Understanding The Stay Behavior

The *stay* behavior is really one of the most important and fun behaviors for lots of reasons. First, all dogs need control, and when training your dog to stay, it really encourages him to watch and focus on you. Another reason that I like teaching it from the very beginning is that this is one of the easier behaviors because the dog is in a neutral sitting position. So if you are looking for something that will get your dog a "win" from the very beginning and build confidence, the stay behavior is great for that.

Elevated areas are essential in teaching the *stay*, because the dog starts on something elevated. As you read about elevated areas, they are a defined place, and I think you will find that they make the training of this behavior much easier.

But the *stay* behavior is a behavior that a number of pet owners get wrong from the very beginning. As a matter of fact, when I tell you the way it should be trained, you might even find you might have made some mistakes in the past.

One of the biggest mistakes people make when training this behavior is thinking they need to call their dog to them after they are happy with the dog staying. If you always call your dog and reward him for coming to you, why would your dog ever want to stay? Think about it from your dog's point of view, because if he is always rewarded for coming to you, that is where he is reinforced.

So here is a good tip. When you are happy with your dog staying, walk to your dog and reward him where he is staying. By doing this, you have now made that area he is staying reinforcing to your dog. A lot of people ask me if it is okay to call their dog to come to them. My response is, of course it is, but remember that is not the *stay* behavior, but it is the *come* behavior. When you are calling your dog to you, that is the "recall" or the *come* behavior. Just remember, when you are working the *stay* behavior, walk to your dog and reward him where he is staying, and if you are teaching the *come* behavior, call him to you.

Starting the "Stay" Behavior

When I start to teach my dogs to stay, as I mentioned, I always use something elevated. I see a lot of dog trainers and pet owners start off trying to "*make*" the dog stay. They say "stay" really loud, are hunched over, and their hand is sticking out towards the dog. And then they take little tiny steps back. If you think about it from your dog's perspective, the trainer is someone looking completely unnatural. By doing these things and thinking you are helping the dog, you are really doing the opposite. If your hand is sticking in his face and you start to step back, you give the dog *a reason to come to your hand.* If you are hunched over and take tiny steps backward, you look very unnatural, and give your dog another reason to come to you.

But if you stand straight, get your hand back, and step back the way you naturally step back, you simply show confidence because you are moving naturally.

So a good thing to remember is instead of "making" him stay in those first few days of training, think more about letting him to "learn" to stay.

- The way you show confidence is through your body language by standing straight and not hunched over.

- If you use a hand cue for the stay (like telling someone to stop), get your hand back next to your shoulder.

- As you step back, do it the way you normally step back.

If every time he jumps off an elevated area that I am teaching him on, he is guided back onto the elevated area, that is a perfect example of that correction being an interruption.

The dog is interrupted, and I give him a chance to try it again. Remember, if the dog is working for a treat or toy for staying, the sooner he does the behavior right, the sooner he gets rewarded. So if we interrupt the dog and give him a chance to try it again, his desire to get the treat or toy tells him, "the sooner I get it right, the sooner I get the reward." And that is why rewards and corrections work hand-in-hand. By the way, that is also a perfect example of using "positive reinforcement."

And one last tip on training: the stay and come behaviors together. If you are stepping back ten feet away from your dog, and you are doing it ten times, you must keep things totally unpredictable. Seven out of ten times you should walk to him and reward him for staying, and three out of ten times you should reward him for coming to you. This way it makes the place he is staying much more reinforcing to him, plus you keep things unpredictable.

Unpredictability

Becoming totally predictable is another trap that a number pet owners, as well as new dog trainers, can fall into. More times than not, the person training the dog has no idea this is happening. There are a few different ways people can become predictable, but the biggest reason is that they simply might have created a pattern they did not realize they created. Although the trainer did not pick up on it, the dog did.

Figure 7 – Knotts Berry Farm, 1986, Buena Park, CA

When you start to become predictable in your training sessions, one of the results that can stem from this is that the dog simply knows what comes next. Predictability is a very common word in the animal behavior world, and especially for those of us who grew up training animals in theme parks in live shows. After performing in every theme park in Southern California, with the exception of Disneyland, in my twenties, I had a chance to see firsthand the results of animals becoming predictable, and what can happen from it. Another name for predictability in live show training environment, is called "show discrimination." Show discrimination simply means you have done a show sequence so many times, that the animal knows what behavior is coming next.

At one point, in some theme parks, we were doing 12–15 shows a day with three different teams of animals during heavy crowd days like the 4th of

Figure 8 - Knotts Berry Farm, 1986, Buena Park, CA

July weekend. When you have animals performing with you in the same sequence of behaviors with the same music, same behaviors, same sequence, and a live audience, you can run into some of the problems just mentioned. The first issue we might start with is what is known as an animal "jumping cues." Jumping cues, as the name suggests, means the animal takes it upon himself to perform the behavior before the cue is given.

If the animal jumps a cue, goes on to do the behavior, and is rewarded, we just created a big problem. Because the animal was rewarded for jumping a cue early, he will not only jump the cue at that point in the show but will most likely to start to do the same thing with other behaviors, at other points in the show. The way we eliminate that problem in a show is to stop the show and have the animal repeat the behavior only when the trainer gives the cue. Unfortunately, we do not want to interrupt the show, so you can see how show discrimination can continue, and build.

The same thing that I experienced in theme parks in Southern California with show discrimination is frequently experienced among pet owners. Because of my experiences back in the 80s, all of my techniques that I currently teach in my dog trainer certification courses involve keeping things unpredictable. There are different times and places where someone can fall into a trap, not knowing he has become predictable, too, but it most commonly happens in a training session.

When you train your dog, do you always do the same sequence of behaviors? Do you ever wonder why your dog keeps going on to the next behavior before you give him the cue? If you ever do a sequence of behaviors, do you ever wonder why the last behavior is the strongest and the first behavior is the weakest?

The answer to those questions is that you have become predictable by doing the same sequence of behaviors over and over without knowing it. You will actually find, if you continue to do this same thing over and over again, something is guaranteed to happen. The last behavior in that sequence is probably going to become a very strong behavior, and the behaviors at the beginning of the sequence are going to begin to breakdown slowly. It's natural because the dog is almost always getting rewarded at the end of the sequence of behaviors.

Think of it from his point of view: Why should he put any effort into a behavior he knows darn well that is not going to be rewarded? People often wonder why some behaviors start to breakdown when they start chaining (more than one behavior), behaviors together. The biggest reason is that they simply have become predictable.

So how do you solve the problem of predictability? It starts with understanding you need to do just the opposite and start becoming unpredictable, so your dog does not know what's coming next. The solution is to:

- Start off by totally changing the sequence of behaviors.

- The second, which is really one of the most important solutions, is to make sure the dog is rewarded at different times during the sequence. Make sure every behavior in the sequence is rewarded at different times.

- Always make sure you change things up. This ensures that predictability does not become a ritual. It will also keep things more interesting for the dog, and not give your dog the opportunity to begin jumping cues.

I hope this chapter has given you a good insight into animal behavior—in particular, personality-based dog training. When you go to train your dog, take the time to develop the relationship, and train your dog according to his personality. Keep the training sessions short and have an idea of what you want to accomplish prior to the training session. Remember that you are only going to teach your dog one part of the behavior during each session, so plan things out. Most importantly, keep training fun, and stay away from creating bad rituals with your dog. Enjoy the rest of the book.

Now let's get into rituals!

CHAPTER 3

Honest & Dishonest Dogs

In 2015, I started talking about honest and dishonest dogs in my seminars and appearances, and I actually teach my students in my dog trainers certification courses about honest and dishonest dogs as well.

When you give a dog a cue to do a behavior, it is not only important you understand how to correct or interrupt the behavior, but it is also important to understand why the dog did the behavior incorrectly. You will learn that there are only two reasons why your dog will do something wrong when you give him the cue. He is either *confused* or he is *testing* you. As you will read, these two variables come into play with dishonest dogs, but they do not with honest dogs. Why is this? Dishonest dogs simply have the natural temperament to want to test you, but honest dogs do not. So let's talk about these two different traits and honest and dishonest dogs.

Duke - 2001

As you start to train your dog, you not only want to take a look at the dog's personality, but you also want to watch how he reacts in the training session. You are going to find that there are some dogs that are 100% direct with their responses—those are honest dogs. What I mean by this is, you will ask them to do something and they will do it, as long as they understand. These are the types of dogs that would never test you. My dog, Duke was that way. At the time, he worked a lot in films and commercials, and he co-hosted Good Dog U with me on Animal Planet, which aired from 1999–2009. He was also one of the top working dogs in Hollywood. One of the things that made

Duke & Joel - 1999

Duke so easy to work with was his burning desire to please. He would never test me—never did in his 12 years. In the 13 episodes that we filmed of Good Dog U, as well as all of the commercials he did, he was 100% into just doing the job and making me happy.

Another interesting thing about honest dogs is that quite often they are yellow dogs. Remember that yellow dogs are laid back in nature and often "go with the flow." It was not a coincidence that Duke was a yellow dog, but he was also that way the day I adopted him from the North County Humane Society in Oceanside, California.

Over my career, I have seen a number of dogs just like Duke that are honest dogs. The characteristics of honest dogs is that they are often very laid back, and extremely easy to teach because of that calm demeanor.

Dishonest Dogs

Okay, so, I am sure a lot of you are wondering what a dishonest dog is, and if it is a bad thing. The truth is, it is not a bad thing, and there are probably more dishonest dogs out there than honest dogs. Most of my dogs were dishonest dogs.

Dishonest dogs are affectionate and love their owners, just like honest dogs. I have seen some of the best relationships between owners and trainers with dishonest dogs. More times than not, a dishonest dog is often a sign of an intelligent dog. These dogs are very quick to learn and to catch onto things.

So, if everything is so great, why do I call them dishonest dogs? These are dogs that often look to take advantage and constantly look for the easy way out. I might actually be describing the dog you own right now. Often times, they will also test you to see what they can get away with. The degree of dishonesty can vary greatly, just like our color scheme you read about in the last chapter.

My dog Foster was a dishonest dog and, at one point, was one of the best working dogs in Hollywood. He traveled with me to over 30 states across the United States, performing with me at seminars, appearances, and conferences. He also made the cover of all four of my books.

In his early days, Foster would test people that would try to work with him through his behaviors. These are the same behaviors I would use when performing with him. If you never have seen me work a dog in front of an audience, I

Foster & Joel - 2010

do a number of behaviors (about 20-30) with my dogs in

random order, always changing. I keep the dog about 20-30 feet away as this is happening. Sit, stay, lie down, play dead, head up, head down, sit up, back up, "cover your eyes," etc.

The point is, if I let someone work with Foster, he would test that person in a way where he would do the opposite of what they gave him the cue to do. If the person said "sit," he would lie down, and if the person said, "lie down," he would sit. If he was in a standing position, and someone gave him the cue to "sit," he would cheat and take about four steps towards that person before he sat (which he knew he was not allowed to do). He would do all this just to see what the person would do! This is what a number of dishonest dogs do, and they do it all in different degrees.

Something I have talked about a lot in recent years is testing and confusion. They both have to do with the reason your dog will do something wrong. Your dog will be incorrect for one of those two reasons: either your dog is testing you, or your dog is confused. That's it! The reason I talk so much about these two variables is because how you deal with each one is totally different from one another. You will find that honest and dishonest dogs come into play here.

Confusion - When your dog is confused, as the name states, he does not understand. A great example is when you train your dog, and you might simply move on to the next step way too fast. We all do it. Most professional dog trainers know when they have gone too fast. The dog becomes confused.

Testing - When your dog tests you, the dog knows what to do; he just does it wrong on purpose. Isn't that funny? Your dog does something wrong, knowing what he is doing is not right. There are a number of reasons for this: some reasons might be boredom, the treat you are using means nothing to the dog, the dog is simply messing with your head, or he's just seeing what he can get away with. Dishonest dogs and smart dogs will do that. The thing that makes a good dog trainer, or good pet owner, is a person who can decipher whether a dog is *testing* or he is *confused*.

As we take a look at honest and dishonest dogs, testing is a non- issue with an honest dog, because he simply does not have the natural temperament to take things to that level. So the great thing about teaching honest dogs is that if they make a mistake, they are most likely confused.

But in the training of dishonest dogs, both testing and confusion come into play. One of the reasons I include this aspect in my seminars, appearances, and books, is because there are so many dogs out there that are dishonest dogs.

In dealing with a dog that is confused, remember that the dog is truly confused most likely because you have progressed too fast on to the next step.

A great example might be if you are training your dog to stay. Let's imagine you have been training your dog to stay for two days from five feet away, and your dog has been consistent. At the end of the second day, you decide to move to ten feet away from your dog. When you back away from your dog and hit that ten-foot mark, he bails from the sitting position and comes to you.

You always need to take a look at the history when your dog makes a mistake, even if it is just the first day of training. In this example the dog is most likely confused because he was consistent from five feet away for two days. It was only when you moved to ten feet away that he got up and came to you. In scenarios like this you also need to take a look at the last step that you made, where the dog made a mistake. Ask yourself if there was a way you could have made the step a bit smaller.

Let's take a look at what happened:

Going from five feet to ten feet is asking the dog to do 100% more of what you asked him to do, and in my world, I believe that is a reach. In any case, there is no question that the dog is confused. The way you handle this is to make it easier, so he understands.

- What I would do is go back to the dog and ask him to stay from five feet away, where he was okay, and reward him.

- After that, I would move to six or seven feet.

- If the dog understood consistently, I would progress in those small increments and eventually get to ten feet.

If the dog is testing you, he is most likely a dishonest dog, and the dog understands what to do. Let's use the same example I just gave you, but now let's make a change. Let's imagine the dog is trained to stay from five feet away but has been doing that consistently for about a week. Nothing in the area that you are training him in has changed, and there are no distractions. At the end of the seventh day of training, you do the same thing you have always done, and now the dog gets up, and breaks his staying position and walks away.

In this scenario, because nothing has changed, and the dog was consistent for about a week from the same distance, there is no question the dog is testing you. If your dog is testing you, there are a lot of reasons why. It can be from lack of motivation by not using the right treat, boredom, or just to see what he can get away with.

- First, I would recommend bringing in a higher value treat than you are using.

- Second, once I had the attention, I would go back to that same five-foot distance and tell him to stay.

- Third, when I told him to stay, I would be a little more firm in the tone of my voice (not yelling).

- Fourth, When the dog stayed, I would walk to the dog and reward him as usual.

You can see by combining these three things, you now have the dog's attention, and one of the biggest reasons for that is the change in motivation. At the same time, you never regressed, and made it easier on the dog. You always remained doing the same thing from the same distance.

Now let's talk about why understanding the difference between testing and confusion is so important. Can you imagine if a dog is truly confused, but the owner corrects the dog for testing? Or if the dog is testing the owner and the owner corrects the dog for being confused?

Let's go back to those last two scenarios. In the first scenario, let's say you had a dog that stayed from five feet away for two days consistently. As you stepped back to ten feet away and the dog bailed from that sitting position, you thought the dog was *testing* you (the dog was truly confused), and the dog was an honest dog.

How do we correct the dog for testing? We repeat the same distance and do not make it any easier on the dog. The only thing is the dog was honestly confused, because he does not have the character to test people. Because of this, there is no way this dog is going to stay from ten feet away, so if the owner continues the training session, the dog will totally fold, and shut down because he does not understand.

You can also see this can be a traumatic experience for some dogs from a mental perspective. Not only will this single training session be a disaster, but I doubt the honest dog will look forward to future training sessions.

Now let's look at the scenario of the dog staying from five feet away perfectly for a week. Again, nothing has changed in the environment. Let's imagine the dog was great at staying from five feet away for a week and broke from the sitting and staying position. There is no doubt the dog is testing you, but you thought the dog was confused.

Remember that if a dog is confused, you want to make it easier, so you are going to move up to two to three feet away next time. That's great for a dog that is confused, but unfortunately, this dog is testing you. Think about this from your dog's perspective, and especially for you out there with dishonest dogs. If you make it easier when the dog tests you, do you think the dishonest dog will try to test again? Absolutely! And, as a matter of fact, you might have just created a huge problem and "let the genie out of the bottle."

My suggestion to all new pet owners that are starting to train their dogs is to take their time and look at history when a dog is incorrect in a training session.

- What does history say, and has the dog been consistent for a period of time? If the dog has been consistent, and nothing has changed in the environment you are training him in, the dog is most likely testing you.

- Ask these questions: Has the dog only been responding to the cue for a short period of time? Have you been progressing through the steps too fast? Has something changed in the environment, or is there an added distraction? If this is the case, the dog is most likely confused.

Can a dishonest dogs be confused? Absolutely! That is why it is imperative you understand why you need to ask yourself the questions above.

Again, if your dog is a dishonest dog, it is actually the sign of an intelligent dog. Remember that dishonest dogs are dogs that have the natural character to want to test you. As you start to train your dog, and you see some signs of testing, you know you need to address those issues right away. If dogs with that personality are allowed to get away with testing early on, there is no doubt they will take advantage and try to test you in a number of other ways down the road.

CHAPTER 4

The Game

When you talk to most successful dog trainers, they will likely tell you that one of the reasons they are dog trainers is that they love what they do, and they love working with dogs. A main factor in dog training is to ensure that the dog trainer keeps the

dog *wanting* to learn. When the dog wants and loves to learn, it makes the job of the trainer that much easier.

Dog training should be perceived as a *game* to your dog. As you read a little farther in this chapter, you will learn that the game can be a number of things that your dog simply likes. Quite often, when it involves dogs that are reactive that are into toys, it can become more intense. In a

Figure 10

number of situations, the game might involve the use of a treat, or high-valued treat. But one thing is for sure, the game is 100% based on the individual dog. The message you want to send to your dog in training sessions should always be "here's the game."

Aside from using treats, the game is really about understanding reactive dogs. If you look at the picture, you will see a

Labrador Retriever that is totally fixed on the frisbee. Nothing will take his eyes off of it. The chance of a dog being more naturally intense or more reactive is based on a number of variables. It is certainly dependent on the individual dog, but another can be the breed of dog the person trains. Another one is based on the personality of the dog and how excited he gets or how reactive he is. The best dog trainers are those who can look at their dog, get to know the animal, and find his or her game.

So when we talk about games, what are we truly talking about? In the world of a human, if you look at Wikipedia, it defines "a game" as ...*a structured form of play, usually undertaken for enjoyment, and sometimes used as an educational tool.*"

Figure 10

I wrote that word for word. It is amazing because that definition of "the game" in the world of dogs is exactly the same. If you look at that definition, it starts off with describing it as "a structured form of play." The most successful dog trainers I have met are the ones that can make training and learning fun and a game, so it is essential the dog looks at dog training as *a structured form of play*. When the opposite happens, and it is no longer a game, and dog training is no longer a structured form of play, the dog is likely to stop looking forward to learning.

The second part of the definition talks about "usually undertaken for enjoyment." Again, you want your dog to enjoy learning, so if the dog looks forward to the training session, then learning becomes something that the dog perceives as enjoyable.

The last part of the definition talks about as an "educational tool." Dogs love to learn and love to please. Being educated and learned is a huge part of most dogs' make-up.

Now that you've had a chance to see *how* the word "game" truly defines dog training, let's take a look at *why* the "game" is so important for every dog owner to understand.

In order for you to understand more about the game, I think it is important to take a look at the breeds of dogs that are out there, to fully understand the variety of dogs' personalities, and the groups they come from.

So, I want to start off by going through some of the most common groups of dogs. For those of you that are not familiar with the world of dog breeding and dog showing, there are seven dog groups. These groups are interesting because in some ways, the dogs are placed in a group based on what they were bred to do. Some dogs, it seems, are placed in certain groups for absolutely no rhyme or reason. So, the seven groups are: the herding group, sporting group, working group, non-sporting group, hound group, terrier group, and toy group.

Figure 11

From these groups, there are four I want to start off talking about. They are the herding, sporting, terrier, and working groups. The reason I want to talk about these four groups, is because they contain a huge percentage of the most popular and most recognizable dogs.

Some of the most common dogs in the herding group covers are Border Collies, German Shepherds, and Australian Shepherds.

Some of the most common dogs in the working group are Boxers, Great Danes, Mastiffs, and Malamutes.

And the sporting group covers almost all of the Setters, Retrievers, Pointers, and Spaniels. This means it covers some

of the most popular breeds such as Golden Retrievers, and Labrador Retrievers.

The last group is the terrier group. This group includes dogs that were bred to hunt and kill and covers a large number of dogs. Some of the most popular being Jack Russell Terriers, Border Terriers, West Hyland Terriers, Miniature Schnauzers, and Soft Coated Wheaten Terriers.

If you look at some of breeds I just mentioned (and there are dozens of others), and if you add

Figure 12

mixes of these dogs in animal shelters and humane societies, these four groups cover a huge percentage of dogs.

If your dog comes from one of these groups, remember that your dog was bred to work. Successful dog trainers will look at

the dog they are training and try to learn about that particular dog's game. So, the dog's breed can play a huge part in all this.

Trying to figure out the game is easier when you have an understanding of what the dog truly was bred to do. Was the dog bred to hunt, herd, or retrieve? What does he like, and is there something he goes crazy over? Remember, you might

Figure 13

have the same breed of dog as someone else, but your dog might like different things, or be more reactive than other dogs.

When we look back at the working, herding, terrier, and sporting groups, most of the dogs will have something in their genetic makeup that drives them to either hunt, herd, or retrieve. That's the game, and the goal for you is to find out what drives your dog. What is it that will make your training session a *structured form of play*?

Figure 14

The reason I wanted to talk about the sporting, working, herding, and terrier groups, is because, even though I like using treats to teach behaviors, there are variables other than treats involved in dog training. If you get to know what your dog truly likes (other than treats), quite often that one thing can be an excellent form of motivation. But there is something else that will increase that drive even more, and that is the "line" of the dog. "Line" or lineage of the dog means the trait and some of the things that his parents, grandparents, and so on were bred for.

A great example is: there are some breeders that will breed dogs strictly for pets, and other breeders who might breed a dog to "work" (to do what he was bred to do). When you see dogs that are bred to work and dogs that are bred to be pets, quite often, you will see a difference not only in their personalities but also in their look as well.

Someone might be looking to find a good quality Labrador Retriever as family pet, and another person might be looking for a Labrador Retriever as hunting dog to work and retrieve birds. These two dogs, even though they both are Labrador Retrievers, will have totally different dispositions.

The working dog is going to have a higher prey drive and be more reactive. Some dogs that are bred to hunt might be more "leggy." When dogs have this higher prey drive, they are going to be more reactive to sights, sounds, and odors.

A Labrador or Golden Retriever that has been bred as a family pet will have less of a prey drive and be less reactive. They also might be a little more stocky and less leggy.

A number of dogs end up being returned to animal shelters and humane societies because the individual or family anticipated that a Labrador Retriever, Golden Retriever, or German Shepherd, or mix would be mellow and a family pet. Yet, the dog they adopted had too high of a prey drive and was way too reactive.

Before a person or family adopts a dog from an animal shelter or humane society, they need to decide prior to adopting the dog, what they are looking for as far as personality and temperament.

It's impossible to know the "lines" of the dog, or the genetic make-up, but there are things you can do at the shelter to test the dog's personality. My suggestion is to experiment with balls or toys if they have them. If you see a dog that is ball or toy crazy and has a higher prey drive, that might work out very well for you if you are looking for a dog that is a very playful or you want to make a working dog. But if you are an older person, or a family just looking for a family pet, a dog that is more reactive might not be the best dog for you.

If you decide to get a dog from a breeder, not only will you want to find a reputable breeder but also a breeder who breeds the type of dog you are looking for. Make sure you find out up front if the dogs are bred to work or if they are bred as family pets.

Remember, there is a huge difference in dogs bred as working dogs and dogs that are bred as pets, and the game is most likely going to be different. Dogs that are bred to work are going to be more reactive and have a higher prey drive, so they are most likely going to be driven by balls and toys. That might be their game. The dogs that were bred as family pets might just have more of a desire for treats, and that might be their game. So, for the dog that is bred to work, the game will constantly revolve around balls and toys. For the dog that was bred as a family pet, the game might be simply working for that treat.

Figure 15

Now that I've had a chance to explain the vast difference in understanding dogs that are bred to work and dogs that are bred as family pets, I want to talk about dogs with a higher prey drive, that are bred to work. Some of the most successful agility and flyball dog trainers will select dogs with a higher prey drive. Almost all of the professional trainers I know are extremely selective in the dogs they choose to train. Ironically, a huge percentage of these dogs come from the herding group. A good example of this is that most dogs you see in agility and flyball competitions are either Border Collies or Australian Shepherds. That's not coincidental. The reason these trainers have figured out these dogs work best is because they understand what their game is. These breeds are simply the best dogs for what the trainers are trying to accomplish, and it all has to do with the way the dogs were bred. They were bred to have a number of ingredients in their makeup that makes them an excellent competitor in the agility and flyball world. They are incredibly athletic, extremely intelligent, and often have a very high prey drive.

Remember what high prey drive means. It simply means that a particular animal will have an increased elevation in the awareness of sights, sounds, and odors. If you talk to any Agility or Flyball trainer, they will tell you that taking a dog that is intelligent, athletic, has a great desire to learn, *plus has a high prey drive* are ALL the makings for a great Agility or Flyball dog.

Those components are not only essential in training agility and flyball dogs, but also crucial in the training of working dogs, such as dogs trained for explosive or narcotics detection, or bite work. So let's talk about those dogs and their game.

The game through the eyes of dogs trained for bite work, narcotics, and explosive detection is driven by one thing, and that is the kill. It comes from the trainer understanding the most reinforcing thing to that particular animal is the kill.

Figure 16

When I talk about the kill, sometimes people get the wrong impression. I am not talking about a dog killing an animal or a person. However there are things the dog can do to play out a number of the actions involved with the kill. As the animal plays out those actions, that is the true "payoff," and that is really what creates 100% satisfaction for the animal.

Figure 17

If you talk to any professional trainer who trains for police work, he or she will tell you one of the most important factors is starting off with the right dog. It is not a coincidence that most of the dog you see are either Dutch Shepherds, German Shepherds or Belgian Malinois. A lot of you reading this book might be familiar with German Shepherds, and they can be great working dogs. A number of you might not have ever heard of a Belgian Malinois, the dog that is pictured. I would like to take a few minutes to tell you about this breed because it is a truly remarkable animal. This breed is one of the most common breeds for police work because their world revolves around working and accomplishing the task.

But there is something more involved, and that is the dog's incredibly high prey drive. The combination of this high prey drive and the dog's willingness to want to please and complete the task, makes this dog the perfect dog for police work. I have had the chance to train this breed of dog before. This dog's intelligence level is incredible, and the drive to learn is second to none. But even though this dog has a high prey drive, and the dog's drive to complete the task is off the chart, there is no question that this breed is not for everyone.

I talked about the payoff earlier, and *the payoff is the satisfaction the dog gets from what he perceives as the kill.* This is one of the most important things to remember when we talk about dogs with a high prey drive that are trained to work. The greater the payoff for the dog, the harder the dog is going to work to get it. This is why if you are going to be training a dog for bite work, narcotics detection, or explosive detection, you are going to want to find the hardest working dog.

Some people think that using treats is the only way to teach a dog a behavior in dog training, but that could not be farther from the truth. Treats are great, and can be a huge part of the game, which I will talk about in a bit. However, using a reward that represents the kill will almost always be more reinforcing to the dog than using a treat. Now let's talk about the kill, and some of the things trainers use to let the dog play out that action.

The Bite

The "bite" is used in a number of ways depending on what the dog is trained to do. A great example is if you see Agility and Flyball dogs go through their routine, after the dog completes the action, he often gets a chance to grab a tug toy or another toy. That action, and satisfaction, is everything to a dog that just completed the action.

The bite itself is a great reward, but even more reinforcing to the dog is what happens after

Figure 18

the bite. You can see right after the dog bites, he then can start to do a number of things, which is what really makes each dog so unique. It begins with the actual bite itself and escalates even more once the dog bites down on the toy. It might start with the dog tugging the toy, or the dog might want to shake it. As the dog tugs on it, he might also start to growl. If you let the dog have the toy, some dogs will shake it even more, and some dogs will actually bring it back to you to continue this game.

Figure 19

In the scenarios I just mentioned, all of those actions not only represent the bite, but most importantly, what happens afterward, which is the kill. The tugging, shaking, and growling represents what happens after the bite. That is what will kill the animal. Shaking the animal will break the animal's neck, and pulling represents tearing the animal apart. If you give a dog something hard like a bone or Nylabone, gnawing on it represents what happens after the kill as well, which is gnawing on the bone. Some dogs are more vocal that others, so with these dogs you might even hear growling combined with these actions. All of these activities represent something to the individual dog; they are a replacement for what the dog would do in the wild.

Now that we talked about some of these actions and their game, let's talk about your dog. Does your dog do any of the actions just described? Does your dog jump up and want to sink his teeth into a toy? Will he tug on it? Will he shake it? Will he bring it back to you? Will he growl as you start pulling on it? If you give him something hard like a Nylabone, will he chew and gnaw on it in a manic way?

If your dog is reactive, he will most likely play out some, or all, of the behaviors just described. The level of excitement your dog will show when playing out these behaviors will vary, and they are based strictly upon his personality and makeup.

With the behaviors just mentioned, it's also important to understand what each one represents:

- Lunging for the object – The behavior of lunging for the toy or object represents the initial bite and attack. This might seem like the actual action, but it is a precursor to what really reinforces the dog.

- Tugging the object – The tugging of the object represents the desire to take "ownership" of what he grabbed after the bite.

- Shaking the object – The animal (toy) that the dog grabbed was not necessarily "dead." That is why the dog often will shake the toy or object, which represents breaking the neck, and the actual killing of the animal.

- Holding the object with his paws – The dog holds the animal (object) down, and tears at it.

- Gnawing on the object – After the animal (toy) is dead, gnawing on the toy or object represents gnawing on the bone of the animal.

Many of you reading this book will find that this does not come as a shock, but for you that have just realized what these actions do represent, I hope it was not too graphic. Now that I just explained this to you, do you see where your dog fits in? Your dog might not have a very high prey drive, so he might not play out any of these actions at all. And your dog might have somewhat of a prey drive and play out some of these actions. But your dog also might have an extremely high prey drive, play out all of these actions, and also be extremely animated as he does so. The thing that makes dog training so much fun is that dogs all have different personalities, and prey drive can vary so much!

The point to all this is to really take the time and get to know and understand your dog. Dogs that have higher prey drives, and that are reactive, need to have these games incorporated as part of their life. Training your dog is another aspect that will help give your dog a job to perform. Take the time to find out the toys and objects your dog loves and keep it fun!

Bite Work

The bite training that we talked about earlier is used 100% of the time when police officers train dogs for bite work. People sometimes think that a dog is just trained to be mad, chase, and bite the bad guy. But professional K9 dog trainers will tell you that could not be further from the truth, that there is so much more to it. The first misconception is that the dog is angry and going after the bad guy. The dog is actually chasing what he perceives as a toy. He is just playing very rough with his toy while using his powerful bite.

The way this is initially trained is, the dog is taught to play with a toy (which can be a number of things). Even though it might be early in the training process, when the trainers are teaching a high prey drive dog, the toy represents the prey and the kill. As the dog is being trained, as the dog lunges and bites, he tugs on the toy, and after a bit of time, the trainer always lets the dog have it. As this is repeated over and over, the dog constantly wins. Any trainer will tell you that the win is essential!

Figure 20

You have to look at this from the dog's perspective:

- He has a natural high prey drive and is inherently reactive.

- The trainer has something that the dog wants.

- He lunges for it and bites it, and that in itself is reinforcing.

- He starts to tug it, which kicks that drive up even more.

- The trainer lets the dog "win" by giving the dog the object.

- The dog will take it and might do a number of things that will play out his action of the "win."

  a) He takes "ownership" of the object.

  b) He might just prance around and show off with the toy in his mouth.

  c) He might hold the toy on the ground with his paws and tug on it.

  d) He might throw it in the air.

  e) He might shake it.

  f) He might bring it back to the trainer.

Now that you understand how a dog's natural prey drive is used in dog training, I want to introduce another word, and that is *agitation*. Agitation in dog training has the same definition as in the human world. If you look at the definition of the word, it will read things like: *to fluster, ruffle, or make nervous*. Although there are some negative results in the human form, in the dog training world there are little to no negative results in using agitation in dog training, with all positive outcomes.

Agitation is used to help increase drive and is used when a trainer teases a dog with a toy or object to create a rise in energy level. If a trainer is holding the dog back on a leash, and another trainer is agitating the dog with the toy or object that he wants badly, this creates drive and anticipation from the dog. The more reactive the dog is, the higher the elevation of drive. Remember we talked about triggers early on, and triggers are precursors. Holding the dog back is the purest form of agitation, because this trigger is what starts everything off.

After the dog is agitated, as the trainer releases the dog

Figure 21

to go after the object, the animal is more apt to exert more energy (as shown) than if the dog were not agitated. That is why using agitation is such an important training tool. You can see by the picture, there is no doubt this German Shepherd is on a mission. His eyes are locked on to where he is going. He plays out in his mind the action that will be happening in just seconds, and he has a burning desire to complete that task.

Over time, police dog trainers start to introduce a replacement for that object they taught the dog with, and that is called a *sleeve*. A sleeve is one of the most valuable tools trainers use for bite work, as it is a replacement for the toy or object. It is something that goes over the arm of a person, that easily slides on and off, and is often made of a burlap type of material that is easy for the dog to sink his teeth into.

Figure 22

What often happens is one trainer releases the dog, and the other wears the sleeve. The trainer with the sleeve will agitate the dog in the exact same way he did with the toy or object while the other trainer holds the dog back. When the dog reaches the sleeve, and gets a good bite, he is rewarded.

He might do a variety of actions as he is biting: he might tug the sleeve back and forth or maybe even tug side to side. Some dogs might do little tugging and just start to shake it right away. Whatever the dog does, this is a payoff, but that is not the end by any means! What the dog does *afterward* is what makes it more reinforcing, and those actions add to the game.

Figure 23

After the bite, the sleeve is slid off, and the dog will do what he needs to do to represent the kill which involves shaking, biting harder, or tugging. Based on their personality, they will do a number of things out of enjoyment.

So, after the sleeve is taken off, you can understand that the act of possessing the sleeve is extremely reinforcing and a huge payoff for the dog. After the dog gets the sleeve, he takes ownership of the "prize," and might shake it, run around with it in his mouth to show off, or maybe even bring it back to the trainer because he simply wants to repeat the whole process. When the dog is finished prancing around with his

Figure 24

prize, he will often lay down with the sleeve. Again, that sense of accomplishment and sense of ownership of the sleeve is the most reinforcing thing for the dog. Time is also a factor. The longer the dog has a chance to lay there and show off his achievement, the greater the reward factor. Whatever the dog does afterward, and it will change based on the dog's personality, is indicative of the dog understanding that part of the "game."

As the dog begins to understand, the trainers will progress to an actual "bite suit," which is a full body suit that is completely padded. Over the course of time, the trainers will set up nearly every scenario they can. This includes running, allowing the dog to watch the person, get released, chase him down, and bite. Although, in the end, what you see is serious stuff; the trainers always teach and train the dog that it is all "a game."

If you want more information on how they train dogs for bite work, I would highly recommend reading more about this incredible style of training written by one of the professionals that have been doing this for a number of years.

The reason I want to teach you about the training, is to show you how the dog thinks, and how big the game can actually become. We will talk later on in the book about how some of these types of behaviors generated by prey drive can work, and also how things can "go south" when you do not realize a game has begun.

As I mentioned earlier in the book, your dog wants nothing more than to be your friend. When that valuable relationship is established, there is no question it helps elevates your dog's drive to learn, and to want to please you. In addition to that, simply using a treat can increase the motivation even more, which is a big help in training behaviors. But using something special

Figure 25

with reactive dogs, something that brings out that drive and increases escalation, is what truly creates the game.

The Game of Treats

Training dogs with treats should always be perceived as a game by every dog. By instilling this principle to every training session consistently, each time you bring your dog out, his attitude will almost always show that increased energy level and a desire to please. During each training session that you take your dog out, he will watch your action and will read loud and clear, "here's the game."

The great news about using treats is that there are a variety of them. Anyone who knows me knows I have been a huge fan of Bil-Jac treats for a long time. As a matter of fact, I know a number

Figure 26

of Hollywood dog trainers that choose to use them also. When I first started using those treats, there was actually only one type and one size, but today things have changed and there are a number of varieties and they now come in a few different sizes. I like using the *Little Jacs*, which is their smaller treats, because they are pretty small. There are times when I plan on putting in six to eight training sessions a day. Anyone who knows me understands I am pretty conservative with the treats, and *Little Jacs* help with that.

Another kind of treat to use would be something made from real food. This might be chicken, turkey, beef, or cheese. Please make sure to check with your veterinarian before you feed any of these foods to your dog and use small amounts.

By using what we call "high-valued treats," which are foods like these, you are given the opportunity to introduce a treat the dog only gets at certain times. High-value treats simply add variation and can really come in handy in situations where you are dealing with "fear" or "anxiety." They should be used sparingly and on occasions where you feel you need a little something extra.

In the last chapter in the book, I will show you how to redirect the dog in a fear environment and will talk about the necessity in using high-value treats. Again, if you can use something that really motivates the dog even more than a normal treat, you will have sent another clear message to your dog in that specific training environment to tell your dog, "here's a new game."

The Right Treat

When it comes to using treats to train dogs, I have seen a lot from pet owners. Over and over again, people train dogs with treats the dog could absolutely care less about. My response is always, "you have one training session and one shot to work the dog today." Instead of using a treat the dog really could care less about, use something the dog absolutely goes crazy over. You want to make sure you always use the treats to your advantage.

The first thing you need to ask yourself, as you are training behaviors using treats, is how many training sessions will you do per day? If you plan on doing a lot of sessions, you will want to really limit the amount of treats you give to your dog. One of the biggest problems I have seen, especially with new pet owners, is that they *over-treat*. This simply means they give the dog way too many treats each time they reward the dog. If you are looking to create motivation and attitude, and something special, it is less likely to happen when you are giving too many treats. You will create motivation and attitude by doing the opposite: by keeping training sessions short and giving small amounts of treats. There is nothing wrong with treating every time when you are training, just make sure you limit the number of treats. If you plan on putting in a lot of sessions, a good tip is to just use some of your dog's dry food to train with also.

As you start to train a behavior, you will want to train each step at a time. As you complete the step, you will move on to the next one. When you complete the last step the behavior is trained.

One mistake that I've seen from owners and trainers is to never make the effort to fade out the treat. Fading out the treat means that you will condition the dog to do the behavior with no treat. If the dog only relies on the treat to do the behavior, over time, he might decide not to do the behavior unless you have a treat. By this happening, you can see that he very easily starts to make his own rules and create his own "game" of only working for the treat. To keep this from happening, you need to start fading out the treat once the behavior is trained. This is accomplished by "pairing" and combining a tactile reward (you pet the dog) with the treat. You want the dog to become conditioned to accept this tactile reward combined with the treat.

- The next step involves you giving the tactile reward 10% of the time by itself, and the other 90% of the time with the treat.

- A few days later you want to start to increase it to 50% of the time with the tactile reward, and 50% of the time with the treat.

- A few days later you should start to increase it to 25% of the time with the tactile reward, and 75% of the time with the treat.

- You can see how you slowly condition the dog to accept the tactile reward. Again, you just create a new game for the dog by *conditioning him* to work the tactile reward.

The Lure Game

Another training technique using the treat is called a lure. It is really one of the most important training techniques, although people often get the training wrong.

There is an art to using a lure, and it starts off with understanding the philosophy behind using the lure.

The first thing you want to do is make sure you know how to hold a treat in your hand. I know it sounds funny, but you can see the right and wrong ways.

The image on the left (below) is the right way to hold the treat. As you can see, the palm faces upward, and the treat is held between the thumb and forefinger. They are both extended out.

The image in the middle is the wrong way, as the hand is facing downward. The dog can barely see the treat. You want to make it as easy as possible for the dog to see and be able to stay in contact with the treat.

The image in the right is the wrong way, as well. The person's palm is facing downward, and he is hiding the treat even more.

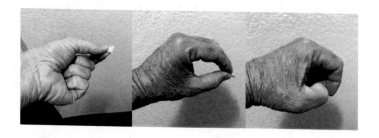

Tip on Luring...

A great tip to remember in teaching the dog to lure is to make sure your dog *always* stays in contact with the treat early on and is rewarded for that. As you make small movements, like moving the treat from side to side, you want to make sure the dog not only follows it but stays in contact with it. Most dogs will do things like lick the treat as he stays in contact with it, which is great!

As the dog begins to understand, you can start luring the treat from side to side, but now as the dog follows it, he might take a step or two.

There is one major mistake people make when learning how to lure the dog. I have actually learned this from teaching my dog trainer certification courses. The mistake is pulling the treat away as they are luring the dog (even a few inches). Once that happens, it is no longer fun for the animal and the dog quits. The game is over. So there really is an art to teaching the dog to stay in contact with the treat. Some people just naturally get it from the beginning, and other people will take a few training sessions to get it right.

The great thing about the lure is that a number of behaviors are trained using it. One of the most common, and most important of all, is the sit behavior. It starts with a lure.

Another behavior that I like to teach within the first week of training is the lie down behavior, and a lure is essential in training that behavior as well. Once your dog has learned some basic behaviors, some of the more advanced behaviors like the play dead, sit up, and crawl are all trained with the help of a lure. So remember, in order to keep it a game, let your dog stay in contact with that treat early on.

As your dog begins to understand to watch the lure, there will be a number of behaviors that can get trained very quickly, as well. If your dog really likes the lure, the sit behavior can often be trained very quickly. When an untrained dog that likes the lure is in a standing position and you want the dog to sit, sometimes moving the treat to three to four feet over your dog's head (shoulder height) will get the dog to sit. This can be a good shortcut for the sit behavior.

Play

One of the most fun games of all, something your dog probably likes more than anything, is to play. Play is something that you can do to simply have fun with your dog, but it's also something that can be used as a reward in a formal training session.

Some dogs play to relax, and some dogs are more intense, and play rough. Remember that no matter what your dog's personality is like, if there is a toy they love, that toy can be used as a reward to teach almost all behaviors.

What is Your Dog's Game?

So the big question is, what's your dog's game? What is it that will create enjoyment for your dog? And most importantly, how can you transform your training technique into a fun and valuable educational tool?

If you can answer that question, I imagine you are most likely having some pretty good training sessions. But if you cannot answer those questions, I hope this book will point you in the right direction. Once you are able to find your dog's game with regards to dog training, you will not only get to truly know and understand your dog, but also enhance your training sessions!

CHAPTER 5

The Human

In order for you to understand some of the rituals dogs might develop, more times than not, there needs to be something that elicits a response from your dog, and that something comes from a human being.

I never really thought much about human behavior with regards to a dog until 2017 and I started teaching my dog trainer certification courses. There is a lot that dog owners do without knowing it. This chapter is all about sharing those things with you. To make it a bit easier to understand, I have separated this chapter into two sections.

The first part, Natural Settings, will go into some of the things you might do on a daily basis around your dog—things that you might not be aware of and may trigger responses.

The second part, Training Environments, will go into some of the things you might do that you do not realize when you are training and teaching your dog.

Movement

I have seen a number of dogs that are great in a variety of environments, around a wide-range of people, places, and things. But the one thing that can trigger a response with a reactive dog might be something moving. I have seen some dogs that could have cared less about anything, yet became unglued when a skateboard went by. A good percentage of dogs that have an issue with skateboards often have that same issue with other moving things or with objects with wheels that make noise. And some dogs might even take it to another level and have issues with fast movement. This means they not only have issues with skateboards, bikes, and things with wheels, but they can also have issues with people simply running past them.

Motion, or movement, is a huge factor in dealing with dogs that are reactive. I cannot tell you how many reactive dogs I have trained that were perfectly fine with other dogs being 20 feet away when standing still with their owners. But once the owners and dogs started to walk and moved parallel, the movement actually triggered the reactiveness.

It's imperative that you understand how much of an impact triggers play to dogs that are reactive to moving objects. Remember that a trigger is a precursor to something happening, and it can be both auditory and visual. The biggest reason for this is that something that is moving does not just appear—often, sounds are involved. The dog gets a chance to hear the person or thing before they appear, and that anticipation is really what can escalate things.

I mentioned that one of the triggers might be something auditory (a sound). If you think about it, your dog's hearing is many times greater than yours. It takes some time for the dog to hear the sound before the object that is making the sound actually approaches the dog. Much like the Fed Ex or UPS person, your dog hears the sound, which is the trigger, long before you do.

I talk a lot about your dog's natural personality because one of the most important things to understand is the dog you are dealing with. Because so many dogs are adopted from animal shelters and humane societies, you may never truly know what your dog's real natural personality is like. The reason is that he might have been in many other different environments or homes prior to you owning him, and people and places have changed as well. But the one thing you can do is to learn and understand from the way the dog is now. This is done by paying attention to his actions and his responses to people, places, and things.

So, when we talk about your dog's natural personality, it is essential you take the time, when you first adopt a dog, to get to know and understand the dog the best way you can. Exposing your dog to people, places, and things can give you a real good look at your dog's natural personality.

Natural Settings

In a natural setting, when people are not training their dog, there are a number of things they might do that they have no idea they are doing, and those things that can elicit a response from their dog. Over the course of time, as their dog gets used to that action or trigger that the person gave, the animal responds with his action, and this action can turn into a behavior pattern and then escalate even further into a ritual.

If those actions that the person performs are larger, depending on the personality of the dog, they will elicit larger responses. In both cases, although they might have started as simple small responses, they can escalate into behavior patterns and habits, too.

But here is an interesting thing. If your dog's response is based on fear, something from his past, or something you have done unintentionally to scare him, it does not take a large action on your part to bring out that fear.

In just the opposite scenario, if the response is based on a dog with a high prey drive and your action involves a toy, again, it does not take a large action on your part to bring out that excitement.

Even though both of those examples come from two totally different ends of the spectrum (fear and excitement), and because they come from such extreme areas on my color spectrum, they don't need a lot from you to bring out that response.

There are two actions that a human will execute that can trigger your dog's fear or excitement—they are sound and movement. If you are dealing with a dog that has a lot of fear, it makes sense that both sound and movement combined are most likely going to generate a more significant response from your dog.

Let's start off with things that you might either do around your house, or things you might handle, that can cause your dog to either become excited or scared. I have listed four totally different examples of things you might do around the house that might increase your dog's fear or excitement:

Skateboards & Moving Objects

I tried to find a place for my moving objects section, and the more I thought about it, the more I realized these are almost always generated from the human. There are many different kinds of moving objects that can trigger responses. One I am very familiar with is skateboards. Moving objects, vacuum cleaners, or loud machines have the ability to elicit a variety of responses from your dog, and these responses can range across the spectrum from excitement to fear.

Vacuum Cleaners

Vacuum cleaners are probably the most common thing in your home that can bring out fear or excitement from your dog. But the vacuum cleaner cannot do this alone, as it must have the help of a human. If you have a dog that is afraid of vacuum cleaners, you continuing to just vacuum will most likely increase the fear in your dog. If this happens regularly, the action the dog plays out can become a ritual. But the interesting thing here is that there are a number of triggers that can play into the dog's excitement or fear. I just talked earlier about sounds and movements, and mentioned when you are dealing with both, it is often more challenging. With vacuum cleaners there are a number of multiple triggers involved, so let's take a look:

- What happens before you start vacuuming with the vacuum cleaner? You turn it on.

- What happens before you turn it on? You plug it in.

- What happens before you plug it in? You let the cord out.

- What happens before you let the cord out? You bring it to an area.

- What happens before you bring it to an area? You take it out of the closet.

- What happens before you bring it out of the closet? You open the closet door.

As you can see, there a total of six different triggers that occur long before you actually start to vacuum. It makes sense that with every trigger comes an increased level of fear or excitement. You can imagine by the time you hit that last trigger of vacuuming, the level of fear or excitement has increased dramatically from the very first trigger of you taking the vacuum cleaner out of the closet. In the last chapter, I am going to show you how to re-train your dog and eliminate these triggers through redirection.

Taking Your Dog For Walks

Walking your dog is something that will almost always increase your dog's excitement level. After all, what dog does not like to go for a nice long walk? Certainly, the response from your dog is not as dramatic as from the vacuum cleaner. One of the reasons for this is that there is only movement involved on your part, and no sounds. So let's see what happens before you actually walk out the door.

- What happens before you walk out the door? You put the leash on the dog.

- What happens before you put the leash on the dog? You might take the leash out of a closet.

- But what happens before that? You must open the door.

In this scenario, although there are multiple triggers involved, they are less than the previous example. Also, the behavior is only based on excitement and not fear, and because of that, it is always easier to deal with. The trigger also involved only movement and no sounds, so there was less of a response from your dog, most likely. Because of the small number of triggers, this behavior is going to be easier to eliminate. I will teach you how to eliminate this behavior in the last chapter.

The Mailman, UPS Guy, or Fed Ex Guy

As you know, anyone who comes to your home or knocks on your door, can elicit a huge response from your dog that usually includes a lot of barking. Over time, this response can manifest into something a lot larger than it originally started with. With people coming to your home, a few of the same similarities to the vacuum cleaner scenario occur, and that's because both sound and movement are involved. The interesting thing about trucks and people coming to your house is that the trigger starts long before you hear the vehicle. But make no mistake, the vehicle is the actual trigger. Like all responses, the longer this has happened, the more intense this behavior can become. Let's look at the triggers:

- Your dog hears the vehicle *long before you hear it.*

- Things escalate as the vehicle comes closer.

- Things escalate as the vehicle appears at your house.

- Things escalate as the person opens the door.

- Things escalate as the person gets out of the truck.

- Things escalate as the person rings the doorbell.

- Things escalate more as the person turns to leave.

Just like with the vacuum cleaner example, multiple triggers, sounds, and movement are involved here. The other thing that can really increase your dog's excitement level is the fact that there is a human involved. Not only are there a number of triggers, but now you might be dealing with a resource guarding issue. So, your dog might also feel like he is protecting the house from the intruder, as well.

Just like the vacuum cleaner example, you always want to start off dealing with the very first trigger.

Feeding Your Dog

There is no doubt that in most scenarios the action of feeding your dog can bring out a lot of excitement. And most of the time, your dog's response will not be as great as with the vacuum cleaner example. But although there are not as many triggers involved, and the result is always excitement, it is worth talking about. Here are the multiple triggers:

- You walk to the closet or garage and take the food out.

- Things escalate, and you pour the food into a bowl.

- Things escalate, and you feed your dog.

Although there are just a few triggers, in this scenario you are dealing with sights and sounds too, and every dog is going to play out a different action as these triggers happen. Some dogs might jump up and down, some dogs might spin around, some dogs might bark, and some dogs might pace.

Rituals When Training Your Dog

Prior to launching my dog trainer certification courses, I never noticed some of the things people did and some of the habits they developed when training and teaching their dog. What's more interesting is that you can tell a person who is learning to train dogs what to do when they are not actually training their dog, and everything can be great. But the second they get in front of the dog and start putting everything into action, their actions can often change dramatically.

If you have read any of my books or seen my TV series, you'll know body language plays a huge part in dog training, and just the mere way you move can play a factor in training some dogs. Based on your dog's personality, sometimes, your body language needs to change.

A good example is to start with red and orange dogs. These are dogs that need a lot of control, so moving quickly around these dogs (especially when teaching the stay behavior) would not be a good move on your part. But when teaching cooler colored dogs like the blues and greens, you can afford to move around a bit quicker simply because you do not need the control you do with the oranges and reds.

Some people's *ritual* in moving around from place to place might naturally be fast. That's simply the way they move because they are a little hyper, much like me! You can get away with that with a cooler colored dog, but you are going to have a problem with training behaviors if you are teaching warmer colored dogs, and especially if you are teaching them to stay.

The same thing applies to a person whose ritual in movement might be naturally slow. Quite often in the training of cooler colored dogs we need to bring out their personality and attitude, so these dogs need us to move around with a little more energy.

As we talk about body language and movement, I see even more interesting rituals that some pet owners develop:

The Stay Behavior

I spend a lot of time teaching the "stay" behavior in my dog training certification classes and have seen three very interesting things people do when training their dog to "stay."

The first thing that people will do is to extend their arm out and hold their hand as if they are telling someone to stop. Well, I do have to say that they are halfway correct, in that they are giving the correct hand cue. The mistake, however, is extending the arm straight out in front of you. As I tell my students, "if your dog is going to bail from the sitting position when you are backing up and telling your dog to stay, having your hand extending out an extra couple of feet is not going to help you."

To train the stay behavior is such a good example, and so much in training a dog involves confidence. In training this behavior, you should not be *making* your dog stay, and instead you should be *teaching* your dog to stay. There is a huge difference.

The ironic thing is your body language can either show confidence or show a lack of confidence when training the stay behavior. To stick your hand out in front of you like that often shows a lack of confidence. Instead, having your hand back almost touching your shoulder is great because you are simply giving the dog a cue, and not trying to force the dog to stay.

Another funny ritual people get into when training their dog to stay has to do with their body movement. When an owner starts to back away from the dog, one of the common things they will do is take very tiny steps backward. I have found in training dogs that you want to do things as natural as possible and stay with your ritual. When you start to move or walk in a way you do not normally walk or move, you raise "red flags" for your dog. Not only does this look funny, but because you are moving in such a different way than you normally move, this movement becomes a trigger to the dog. So, instead of taking those tiny steps, I teach students to take longer strides when backing away from their dog. If you think about it, most people naturally take longer strides as they are naturally backing up, so this looks totally natural.

One last thing people will do when training their dog to stay, and start stepping back, is to be hunched over. I really think the "hunched over" thing is usually combined with the arm sticking straight out. The owner thinks their hand is closer to the dog, so in the owner's mind, he thinks the dog is more likely to stay. You want to make sure you stand the way you normally stand (that would be straight) and not hunched over.

So, if we combine these three things, we have the owner taking short, tiny steps backward, standing hunched over, with his hand is sticking straight out in front of him. As you can imagine, this looks as funny as it sounds. If this is something you do when you teach your dog to stay, you can see why your dog would be more apt to break from the stay position.

But the reality is that because this is something that looks strange and different to your dog, and is something you always do when you teach your dog, you have now created a certain ritual around your dog. Remember, by doing something different in a training session, something that is totally altered from the way you normally act and move, this can trigger your dog to act in a certain way. In this scenario, his action would most likely be breaking from the stay position.

So don't let what I just described become your ritual. Be aware of what you are doing and catch bad habits early!

Lie Down Behavior

The way I teach the lie down behavior is to start with the dog in a sitting position. I like to keep one hand on the dog's shoulder blades, and the other hand with a treat below the dog's mouth. I condition the dog to take the treat from that position and slowly start to bring my hand toward the ground. This will eventually get the dog to take the treat from the ground. Some dogs will lie down and others will be in a slouched position to take the treat, which is okay. For the dogs in the slouched position, over the next few training sessions, I start slowly move my hand along the ground towards me an inch at a time. Over the next few training sessions, this will get the dog to lie down.

Here is where people can develop a bad habit or ritual. It is essential when you slowly begin to move your hand to the ground that you move it directly to the ground in line with your dog's lower jaw. The mistake that a number of owners make is to guide the dog on an angle towards them. When this happens, I guarantee that your dog will stand, and you will have to repeat what you just started.

Tip: So that this does not become a ritual for you, always make sure to slowly guide the dog toward the ground by putting the treat directly below his lower jaw. Make sure the direction is towards the ground, and do not pull the treat towards you until the back of your hand is on the ground.

Understanding How Voices Have an Impact

Your voice has a huge impact on how your dog reacts to you. As a matter of fact, your voice can actually trigger a number of reactions. Quite often, those reactions become habits or rituals. One of the most common reactions I have seen comes from red or orange dogs is when people first come in through the front door. If you have a dog that likes to bark or get excited when guests come over, there are things you can to do to either increase or decrease the dog's barking and excitement level. Obviously, the goal is to do the latter.

Voices play a huge factor in this. I am sure you've seen a situation where people enter a house and the dog starts to bark. At the same time, there might be someone that just walked in that immediately will start to play with the dog while using a high-pitched voice. Most people that have been in this situation know this is not the greatest way to eliminate the barking and excitement. As a matter of fact, you are more likely to assure the barking will continue with this kind of trigger coming from the human's side.

If you can understand that high-pitched voices, often times, increase the dog's level of excitement, then using a lower, more firm tone is more likely to do the opposite, and that is to decrease the energy level of the dog. Now you have an understanding of how your voice can have such a huge impact on either increasing your dog's excitement or calming your dog down.

I hope this chapter has given you a better understanding of some things that people do that can be triggers for improper behavior. These actions that your dog play out can happen both in training sessions or in times when the dog is just sitting around. Be aware of your actions.

CHAPTER 6

Fear & Excitement

Earlier in this book, you learned about my color spectrum, and particularly about the cooler colored dogs. You learned the goal was to get your dog to move towards the center of the color spectrum. The closer your dog is to the center, the easier your dog will be to train. At the same time, if you do not train and socialize some dogs, they can move away from the center of the color spectrum. Once that happens, it makes things more challenging.

You learned the green and blue dogs can range on the color spectrum from a dog that is just cautious and apprehensive to a dog that is very afraid.

You also learned about the orange and red dogs that are the warmer colored dogs, and that the red dogs can be more reactive.

When orange dogs are given the opportunity to consistently be in environments that increase their reactiveness, and given the ability to play out the excitement, the behavior can unfortunately become a pattern, and eventually a ritual. This is how orange dogs can go red.

Although the warmer colored dogs and the cooler colored dogs come from totally different ends of the color spectrum, they both can develop behavioral issues that originate from their natural character and make up. Those personalities have to do with fear and excitement.

A green dog, that is cautious of a certain person, needs to be exposed and desensitized to that person. If the dog is desensitized early, the dog can go yellow. If not, as you saw in the color spectrum, the dog can go blue.

The same thing applies to the orange dog that gets excited over a person. The orange dog needs to be exposed and desensitized to the person that is causing the excitement. If the dog is desensitized early on, and the problem is dealt with, the dog can go yellow. If not, the dog can go red.

In this chapter we are going to separate it into two parts, and they are fear and excitement. The thing new pet owners need to understand before they bring a dog home, whether the dog is from an animal shelter or breeder, are two important aspects of dog training: socialization and desensitization.

Socialization and Desensitization

I really enjoy talking about these two aspects of dog training for a number of reasons, but the biggest is that all dogs need exposure. When exposing dogs, I teach all new students there is a huge difference between socialization and desensitization, so you want to make sure you do not confuse the two.

Socialization simply means you take a new dog that you perhaps have just brought into your home, and get him used to people, places, and things. This dog you are socializing has *no known fears or anxieties* over people, places, or things that you know of. But one of the ways to find out if your dog has some sort of fear is to get the dog out and learn about the dog. As an owner socializes their dog, the dog becomes used to people, places, and things. Time is everything when you are socializing your dog too, so the more time you spend getting your dog used to all these distractions, the better your dog will be around them.

A good example of socialization is when I first get a dog from an animal shelter that I am going to want to train for movies and commercials. One of the first places I will go to is the grocery store, and I will stand about 10 feet away from the automatic doors that open and close. I feel like those are best distractions because they offer both sights and sounds. This location gives you the audio and visual aspect of the doors opening and closing, and you have the visual aspect of a variety of people coming in and out of the doors.

I will start with the dog about ten feet away from the doors. Most of the time, by the next day, I can move to about four or five feet away. At that same time, because the dog is now starting to get used to the people, I can now ask them to give the dog a treat.

If you think of this from the dog's perspective, getting a treat from everyone from all ethnicities, old and young, male and female, creates a situation where the dog sees everyone as a positive thing. As the dog gets more comfortable in that environment, I can move up next to the opening and closing doors, while I am constantly having people feed the dog a treat. Over the course of a week, in most cases, the dog totally gets used to this environment.

Think about this. If from the very beginning of bringing your dog home, your dog can get used to loud doors as they open and close, people coming in and out, and look at everyone as a positive thing, you are on the right track! The greatest part about getting your dog used to this environment is that this lays a great foundation in getting your dog used to other environments. Remember that the same steps you used at the grocery store can be applied to every other environment in which you want to socialize your dog.

Desensitization

Desensitization is much different than socialization. Desensitization means you get your dog used to a known person, place, or thing that scares or excites the dog. Desensitization can be used with dogs with a variety of personalities. In a number of cases, this involves a cooler colored dog having some sort of fear or anxiety of a person, place, or thing. But it can also involve a warmer colored dog like an orange or red that just gets extremely reactive and excited over a person, place, or thing.

A good example of this elevated reactiveness might be a person on a skateboard that excites the orange or red dog. Either way, when we desensitize an animal to something, we almost always find a way to redirect the dog away from the person, place, or thing that either excites or scares him. We will show you how to deal with that behavior problem in the next chapter.

Barking

Barking is probably one of the most common natural rituals. This behavior gives your dog a way to express himself. As we talk about fear and excitement, barking is simply a way of communicating his different feelings of happiness, enjoyment, concern, fear, or panic.

Dogs bark as a form of excitement, but they can also bark as a form of fear or panic as well, so the action of barking can be a way of expressing many different attitudes or feelings. There are three different temperaments dogs will have when they are barking:

- Fear – Dogs will bark out of fear, and many of the times the barking will be combined with the dog's body language which might involve backing away, or maybe even hiding behind a person, place, or thing.

- Pure excitement – Dogs will also have their own way of expressing they are just happy! And this barking just expresses his enjoyment, and often occurs when you come home. Quite often this barking will be combined with the dog's body language of spinning around, jumping left to right, or just moving around you.

- Aggression – With aggressive barking (not out of fear), the dog is expressing his desire to go after the person, place, or thing in an aggressive manner. You might see this when the dog is on a leash barking, and you might also see this when a dog is behind a fence. The barking often comes from the frustration of not being able to go after what he has developed the aggression over.

Now that I've laid out the three different kinds of personalities that will accompany the barking, you can see that it is very important to figure out why the dog is barking. If the dog barks out of excitement, that's great. You can still get rid of the problem, but at least you know why the dog is doing it. But in a situation where the dog barks out of either fear or aggression, those issues need to be dealt with, and always by a professional who has experience in dealing with fear or aggression.

Fear

Fear is a huge issue that many new pet owners will deal with when adopting a dog from an animal shelter or humane society. Green and blue dogs will have the natural character or makeup to be fearful.

COLOR SPECTRUM X

MORE CHALLENGING >>>>>> EASIER <<<<<< MORE CHALLENGING

Because these dogs come from so many unknown environments, nobody truly knows why the dog is afraid, so it is always a challenge to find out what is exactly frightening a dog, and more importantly, what the trigger is.

When you train a green dog that is timid and apprehensive, things will always be easier than dealing with a blue dog that is extremely afraid or scared of a person, place, or thing. The difference in these two colors of dogs is that the fear in the blue dog has, in most cases, escalated and already become a habit or ritual. In most cases, the green dog is still apprehensive, and because of that, training can be very successful.

After dealing with a number of problem-solving issues over my dog training career, there is no doubt I enjoy trying to solve some of the issues that deal with fear more than any others.

The one thing I always tell my clients when they adopt a dog is to socialize the dog from the very beginning. As we talked about earlier in the book, the closer your dog is to the center of the color spectrum, the easier your dog is to train. A yellow dog, most likely, has no fears or anxieties. Because he is so laid back, very few things will scare him. A green dog is timid and apprehensive, and a blue dog is extremely afraid or scared. The ritual of fear has most likely already started with the blue dog. But you can work with a blue dog, and in time he can go green.

In understanding fear and apprehension, you need to first understand that we are talking about an animal and not a human being. I know that sounds funny, but I have had a number of conversations with pet owners over my career and have made that very same statement. People often want to anthropomorphize (give human reasons for animal's responses) on why an animal is afraid of a person, place, or thing. The reason an animal might be afraid of something, and the reason a human might be afraid of something can be extremely different. Below is a good example.

Let's start off discussing an animal we train for movies and commercials. It is not a dog. When we train cats for movies and commercials, we do not just have one cat. Instead we have a team of cats; kind of the same way actors have stunt doubles. Typically there are two to three cats that look alike per team. So when a production company pays for a cat, they get the whole team for that entire day. I have seen some great working cats, and I have even had the opportunity to train many cats as well.

Professional cat trainers will tell you what I am about to tell you. As great as some of these cat teams are, they are much different than a human in how they remember things that they perceive as a negative experience, or a situation that scares them. An example is when we work on the set. Although we take a lot of precautions, there are rare times when something might fall 10–20 feet away from where the animal is, or even an accidental loud sound might scare the cat.

What I have seen in the past is, we can have a team of cats that have worked on the set for ten years, but if there was something that scared one of them eight years ago, that event is always foremost in the cat's memory. They often do not forget things like that. People are different in that we can forget many negative experiences from two to eight years ago.

The reason I brought up this example is because dogs can be the exact same way when it comes to fear. If there was an experience that happened with a dog years ago, and it really had an impact on him, it is sitting right there in his memory, most likely. The closer your dog is to the center of the color spectrum, the less of an impact that event will have. But the farther away from the center of the spectrum, the more of an impact that event will have.

Now that you know this, you can see that when people adopt dogs from animal shelters and humane societies, a number of these dogs have baggage, and much of the baggage is unknown. That it is why it is essential to socialize your dog from the very beginning, so that you might be able to get an idea of things that might scare him. Remember, if your dog has a fear of something, it can be related to both something that happened recently and something that happened years ago.

> Triggers - In dealing with fear or an apprehension to a person, place, or thing, there is almost always a trigger, or a number of triggers involved, as we talked about early in the book. A trigger is simply a precursor that will elicit the dog's fear. As mentioned, quite often, many pet owners are not aware of this trigger until after the behavior has escalated into a habit or ritual.

> Multiple Triggers – A number of different triggers can be precursors to something that might scare an animal. Sometimes it might just be one trigger that will cause the fear, and other times it might be a number of back-to-back triggers, which are multiple triggers. Quite often, the more triggers, the more the fear or excitement has the ability to escalate.

Fear of People

An example of a single trigger might be a person. If the dog is afraid of the person, the fear comes from that person and nothing else. But there are a number of things that person might do that can escalate the fear even more. One thing that can cause an escalation can come from the person's movement. Other variables might include what that person is holding or maybe the way he looks directly at the dog.

Fear of Other Dogs or People on Walks

I have found in dealing with fear of a person when walking your dog, and fear of a person when you are in your home, your dog's response being very different. One of the reasons is, when you are out on a walk, your dog might show you more of a variety of responses that show the fear or apprehension. If you are walking your dog and he is afraid of a dog or person that is walking across the street, there will be one of three actions he will manifest that will show that cautiousness or fear.

- He might continue walking, but slow down as he watches the dog or person

- He might come to a complete stop and stare

- He might immediately get behind you and stare

You can see with the three instances, there is no doubt the dog is concerned about the other dog or person, but the good thing is you are able to see your dog's response at an early stage of ownership.

- You might have a situation where your dog is concerned about the dog or person, but he continues to walk. This lets you know the dog is concerned about the person or dog, but not enough to stop walking.

- You might have another situation where your dog is so concerned that he comes to a complete stop and stares. This lets you know the dog is concerned enough about the person or dog that he comes to a complete stop.

- You might have another situation where the dog is so concerned that he hides behind you. This lets you know that the fear of that person or dog has really accelerated.

Becoming aware and understanding your dog's body language when it comes to fear of people and dogs early on, is one of the most important things you can do for your dog. You can see that, although these three examples all involved the fear of a person or dog, the examples differed in the degree of the fear. The first example will be easier to deal with, the second example will be more challenging, and the last example will be even more challenging than the second.

As you have read this book, I hope you might have already seen some things you have never been aware of that have caused your dog to be scared. Once these things are identified, the next step is to pay attention to your dog's behavior. Remember, by being aware, you will start to learn about some of these triggers, and how they can cause the fear to manifest and build. Most importantly, in the last chapter, I will show you how to use redirection to deal with unwanted behaviors, habits, or rituals.

Reactive Dogs & Excitement

Over-excitement is another issue that a number of new pet owners might have to deal with when bringing a new dog into their home. These behaviors are totally opposite of what you just read about with the green and blue dogs. This excitement will most likely involve your warmer colored dogs which are orange and red. However, you might have a blue dog that can become orange with certain triggers.

With dogs that get over-excited or become highly reactive, a number of behavior problems can develop and become rituals. A good example of some behaviors that will stem from excitement is a dog that wants to mouth a person or jump on people. This mouthing, which is sometimes a form of testing, over time, can accelerate into snapping, growling, and biting. When the mouthing is combined with the jumping, it can often increase the energy and excitement level greatly. So remember, a behavior that starts off with a dog that does not listen and just plays rough, can often turn into something much worse. This also can escalate into dogs that do not listen and try to take advantage of people. A smart dog that begins to ignore you and stops listening might use that as an excuse, and as a way of taking control in a variety of other situations.

Humans & Excitement

As you learned from chapter one, the greatest thing about training dogs is the fact that their personalities cover almost every color of the rainbow. Dogs that are red or orange (warmer colored dogs) are likely to be naturally more reactive than green or blue dogs (cooler colored dogs). We discussed the fact that dogs can change colors as well. There are a number of dogs that are naturally green that can become orange or red (reactive) when put in an environment where something is present to increase the prey drive of that dog. If there is a change in the environment, it almost always is altered by a human.

Earlier in the book, you also had a chance to learn about things that can naturally trigger excitement in your dog. In chapter 3, *The Game*, you learned that some things humans do can bring out the excitement and actions that the average pet owner might not necessarily want. Actions like heavy play with certain breeds of dogs, and dogs with high prey drive, can become the ultimate reward for that particular dog. The truth is, the only way those behaviors can develop with that magnitude and level, is with the help of a human.

When humans are introduced to the equation, the dynamics can change, and that person can also be responsible for allowing unwanted behaviors to escalate. You will also find that it really does not matter the personality or color of the dog, either. Unwanted behaviors are not color-specific, and both orange and green dogs can develop bad behaviors. Just like we have talked about in this book, excitement that is allowed to escalate and build up, can become a pattern or ritual. Once rituals are established, getting rid of the behavior is much more difficult.

Understanding Your Dog

In the chapter, *Animal Behavior*, I talked about taking the time and getting to know your dog. I mentioned that there were three steps to that:

- Getting to know your dog

- Developing a relationship

- Building the trust

In the "getting to know" phase, I talked about taking the time to get to know the things your likes and does not like. I want to focus on the things your dog does not like. When you get to know and understand your dog, and if he came from a humane society or animal shelter, it's quite possible there will be some things he does not like. If there is a person, place, or thing he does not like, he is going to show you this in a variety of different ways.

In the last chapter, I will show you how to interrupt some of the most common behaviors that are generated out of excitement.

Aggression

I am by no means a specialist in dealing with aggression, but I do understand aggression and have eliminated aggression in a number of dogs over my career. In addition, I personally know some of the best dog trainers in the United States that are specialists in dealing with aggression.

With a number of aggressive issues, there are two factors that will almost always come into play.

- The first has to do with the dog being possessive in some way. The aggression most likely started off with the dog being possessive in some sort of manner over a person, place, or thing.

- The second factor has to do with a human being. The dog might be possessive *of* that person. This means he will guard and protect that person. He might also have an aggression *toward* a person or people.

- When we talk about a dog being possessive over a person, place, or thing, there is a term that is used frequently in the dog training world and that is *resource guarding*. This ritual of possessiveness might very well start off as something natural, and can manifest and build into snarling, growling, or biting. In almost every case, the human that owned the animal most likely missed a trigger or behavior early on. The trigger that was missed enabled the dog's response to build and grow, and quite often, this is what led to a serious behavior problem.

You have heard the word *escalation* a lot in this book, and you have also heard the expression *allowed to manifest*. When we talk about things like resource guarding, in most cases, if the behavior was caught early, the behavior would not have been able to escalate or build into something serious.

Not every dog has the character or makeup to be possessive over something. The truth is there are a number of dogs I have adopted over my career and trained for film and TV, from animal shelters and humane societies that had no natural resource guarding behavior instinct whatsoever. The few dogs that resource guarded were ironically both orange and green dogs. This means that resource guarding is not color specific, so it can occur with dogs that have a higher prey drive, as well as dogs that have little or no prey drive at all.

When you adopt from an animal shelter and humane society, it is highly likely you will never truly know the dog's history. A dog that shows signs of a resource guarding behavior may have that trait naturally, but most likely, it will be the result of something that happened with the previous owners at one time or another. Dogs that are allowed to become possessive over people, places, and things, and get away with it, will only view that as reinforcement. As this happens, things continue to escalate. This is why the human is often a huge factor in all of this.

I have always said, and especially in chapter nine of *More What Color is Your Dog?* book, "the completion of the bad behavior is a reward." Allowing your dog to play out actions you do not want, can be extremely reinforcing to your dog. Because of that, the behavior will continue to intensify. It is up to the person or family that owns the dog to be aware and not allow these unwanted behaviors to increase. If they do, they can become rituals.

It is a good idea, when you bring in a dog from an animal shelter or humane society, to see if your dog has this natural desire to resource guard. There are a few simple ways to see that behavior, so I would try this after your dog has had some time to get comfortable in his new home.

When you test, the most important thing is that you do not want to do anything that will make the dog uncomfortable. The last thing you want to do is get bitten. What you are looking for is body language from your dog. If the behavior is going to happen, most of the time it will happen when you are as far as four to eight feet away.

The best way is with a bowl of food. Take a bowl of food, set it down, and let the dog get comfortable eating. You want to start off by walking casually towards the dog from about six to eight feet away. As you walk a bit closer, and get three to four feet away, stop and watch his body language, because there are two things that are going to happen:

- Some dogs will totally ignore you and continue eating

- Some dogs will stop eating

If your dog stops and looks at you, stop where you are, and take a look at his body language again.

- His body language might not have changed at all, and he might just stop and look at you and stands the way he was while eating.

- But his body language might have changed dramatically. He might have put his head down towards is bowl, while staring at you through the corner of his eyes.

- His hair around his shoulder blades might stand up, which is a behavior that's called "being hackled" or "hackling." Hackling is a sign of excitement that can happen when a dog is playing. It can also occur when a dog is showing aggressive behavior.

- Another behavior to look for is the front legs spread out a bit. That, combined with the other behaviors mentioned, is another sign a dog is being possessive.

- Snarling or growling are probably the most obvious of all behaviors that might show a dog being possessive.

If your dog just ignores you, you might want to move a bit closer and stop. Do not bend down, and do not reach for the bowl. He might play out one of those actions when you get a bit closer, and the dog might do one of those actions when you are as close as a foot away.

So, the question is, did anything happen? Did your dog just ignore you? If your dog ignored you, that is great. If your dog did react to you:

- The first question you want to find out is where does it happen?

- Does it happen from six feet away?

- Does it happen at one foot away?

These are important questions to ask because the distance plays a very important part of the equation. If your dog lets you get a foot away before he plays out an action, this indicates that you are able to walk to a pretty close distance from the dog before the action happened.

On the other hand, if the behavior happened from six to eight feet away, you did not need to be close to the dog for the behavior to happen. If your dog reacted to you being six to eight feet from the bowl, there is a good chance that the behavior has escalated, and you need to have someone who deals with aggression help you with the problem.

However, if the dog let you come all the way to the bowl before it happened, it tells you the behavior has not progressed to a severe problem yet. I would still recommend a specialist with aggression coming in, but you know it is not as serious as the prior example.

Even though I have trained dogs for many years, as I mentioned earlier in the book, I am not a specialist on dealing with aggression. If you have any issue where a dog is acting unusual around food, treats, or food dishes, please make sure you contact a dog trainer that specializes in dealing with aggression.

Using this example, you can see that a dog can be naturally possessive from the very beginning. If your dog has lived in an environment where his prior owners either did not know how to deal with that behavior or allowed it to happen, you are going to deal with a resource guarding issue.

Dogs cannot only be possessive of food, but also naturally possessive of a variety of people, places, and other things.

Resource Guarding & People

When we talk about resource guarding associated with people, I've seen two different situations. The first is a dog that becomes protective of a certain person, which most of the time is the owner. The other type of resource guarding is the kind where the dog's aggression is directed at a certain person or people. These are two totally very different scenarios.

In the first example, a dog that becomes protective over a certain person is performing an action that makes him feel comfortable. You might see a dog that either growls, snaps, or bites when someone comes near the person that is holding him.

I have seen this behavior happen with dogs from all colors of the spectrum, but it is most common with green or blue dogs. These are animals that are already cautious and insecure, and now a person or thing has been brought into the equation that has made the dog even more afraid. So because of this fear, the dog often feels the need to protect the one person he feels comfortable with.

As a dog continues to become possessive of that person, and he is able to play out the action, that action becomes reinforcement to the dog, and can become a ritual. If you think about it from the dog's perspective, he is uncomfortable with someone who approaches him and his owner. He does something like bark or snap, and the person that was approaching withdraws himself. Because no one corrected or redirected the dog, and the dog was able to complete the action, in his mind he is rewarded. As this happens over and over again, the dog is most likely going to do it again. The more times he does this, the more this behavior has the ability to escalate.

In addition, there is no doubt that dogs who resource guard are also very smart dogs. I think most owners who have dealt with these kinds of dogs likely will agree with me. As you read earlier, one of the signs of a smart dog is a dog that likes to test people. Dogs testing people and people testing people are no different. They both are trying to see what they can get away with. Not only will a dog become possessive over their owner, but the dog will soon begin to feel like he is in charge if no one is there to either correct or redirect him for becoming possessive over the person. As this happens, smart dogs will often start trying to take charge of other situations as well.

A good example of taking charge is a simple thing like when you try to put the leash on the dog. We will imagine you own a very smart dog that has done some resource guarding over a person, but no one has corrected the dog.

Now let's say you want to take the dog out for a walk, and as you reach for the collar and touch the dog's collar to attach the leash, he softly starts to growl at you. Because you were caught off guard, you naturally pulled your hand away before you were able to attach the leash. So think about this from your dog's perspective. You go to attach the leash, he performs an action that says, "don't do this" and instead of putting the leash on, you do not follow through with what you had planned to do. He wins. If your dog is able to play out the action, he is reinforced. Most importantly, with dogs that are possessive and are constantly able to "win," they will continue to dictate, and the bad behaviors are most likely to escalate. This means that a dog that wants to take control, and is successful, will often begin to take even more control.

A dog that growled, might actually begin to nip or bite. A dog that snapped, might become more serious with the bite next time. In dealing with any behavior problem that revolves around resource guarding or a dog becoming possessive over a person, place, or thing, you need to not allow that action to play out by the dog. This starts with good training, and most likely bringing in a professional that specializes in dealing with aggression.

The Solution

In order to not let your dog play out the action, you will want to interrupt the behavior. To do that, there are a number of training tools a good trainer will help you choose. In the last chapter, I will go into some ways you can use both redirection and interruptions in resource guarding cases that are still in the early stages.

If, for some reason, the behavior has escalated or you feel has become a habit or ritual, and you decide to bring a trainer in, *please* make sure to select a trainer who has experience in working with resource guarding issues and, most importantly, in dealing with aggression. ***Do not*** bring in a trainer or animal behaviorist who tells you they are going to use treats, or they are going to "ignore" the behavior to get rid of the problem, because it will *not* work in dealing with most advanced resource guarding or aggression issues.

Anxiety

Anxiety is a behavior that varies immensely in dogs. I have seen cases of nervousness that were totally trained out of the dog in a few sessions. I have also seen extreme cases where the dog actually got better but never would be normal. I have also seen a number of anxiety issues that were brought on by the previous living environment. Sometimes the lack of previous animal care, or the way the dog was trained in the past, created a real challenge for the family that just adopted a dog from an animal shelter or humane society. There is a word I like to use with dogs that have this behavior problem: I call it abandonment. Many people call it "separation anxiety." Often, this abandonment becomes so escalated and so severe that it becomes a ritual. Sometimes, if a dog has lived in an environment of abandonment, has been abandoned, or feels abandoned, and is adopted by someone who loves the animal and cares for him, they can create a great bond. But what I have also seen is, because of the history of abandonment, the dog can become "glued" to that person.

I have seen a number of cases like this where the person literally cannot go anywhere, because the dog is so co-dependent on the person, he is now afraid of being abandoned. There are even times where the anxiety is so severe that every time the person leaves, the dog tears the house apart. I have also seen situations where the owner tries to use a crate to limit the dog from destroying things, but the dog still gets injured in the crate.

When dogs have anxiety issues, there is almost always an escalation. If you own a dog with anxiety issues, and you leave your home, you most likely know what I am talking about.

If you own a dog with anxiety issues that is loose in your home when you leave, based on the degree of the anxiety, a number of things can happen.

- When you leave, the first thing your dog is most likely to do is start to pace as he looks for you.

- Accompanied with the pacing might be some whining too.

- As the dog begins to create even more anxiety and nervousness, he might begin to pace even faster, and the whining might turn into barking.

- As things begin to escalate, the dog might start to move around even faster in a manic way and might start to use his paws to dig at the door.

- And as things escalate, even more, you might even see the dog bark loudly, run around extremely fast, and dig at the door more frantically with a lot of energy.

With the explanation above, you can see that often escalation plays a big part of a dog's anxiety issues. In some instances where it might still be in the early stages, not giving the dog the opportunity to play out those actions can certainly work.

We will talk about how to deal with this issue in our last chapter, but most trainers will tell you there is no one cure, and that it is all based on the individual dog. If your dog has anxiety issues, I would always suggest starting with a trainer that has experience dealing with anxiety problems. If, for some reason, the problem has escalated to where other things might be needed and training does not help, I would highly recommend talking to your veterinarian.

Fear Aggression

Fear aggression is by far the most common form of aggression. People that do not understand dog training might hear the word fear aggression and think that it might be something that is not as serious because of the word "fear." It is a huge mistake to think like that that. Any trainer that has dealt with aggression issues will tell you that fear aggression is not only the most common form of aggression, but also something that needs to be dealt with immediately.

I want to spend some time talking about dogs that that have a need to play out fear. To have a dog send you a message (such as barking) that he is not comfortable with a person, place, or thing, is actually something you want to see. Remember that the dog is simply letting you know that a person, place, or thing is causing him to be fearful and have some sort of anxiety.

If you look at the color spectrum, you will see the green dog. A green dog can be timid and apprehensive, but that green dog can turn blue if not socialized, not trained, or not properly cared for. Professional dog trainers see this a lot, as a green dog can go the wrong direction and can become extremely fearful. The result of a blue dog becoming fearful will deteriorate into a very dangerous situation as he can become "fear aggressive."

I have always used the expression *kill or be killed* when I talk about how I perceive the blue dog with fear aggression and how he sees the world at the particular instant he becomes afraid. This means the dog has exhausted everything, and now he is left to do what he perceives will help him live, which is bite at what is causing him this great fear.

It really is a sad thing to think about, and to consider this dog's life, and what he had to endure for so long that got him to this place.

I like to use different examples when I explain to audiences how the fear might begin, how it can build, and how it can spiral out of control into serious fear aggression.

One of the examples I like to use is a situation in which a family owns a "blue" Cattle Dog. We know these types of dogs are working dogs and are known to have a higher prey drive, which means this breed is probably going to be more naturally reactive.

A family owns this extremely afraid and nervous dog. His favorite place is in the bedroom in his bed next to the family's bed. Even though he spends a lot of time in his bed, when the dog gets nervous, he runs to the bedroom as he knows his safety net is his bed. His ritual has become the security of his bed.

They have a few kids, and their youngest son is five. The son understands this dog, and the family has told him to not chase, or corner the dog. But today the son had a birthday party with ten other kids coming over, all being the same age. The dog is loose in the house, roaming around cautiously and hears a lot of running around and screaming, which already elevates his nervousness. As nobody is paying attention because they are busy with the party, a few kids see the dog, and start moving toward the dog. As they do, this the dog runs down the hallway into a room at the opposite end of the house from where his bed is located. As the dog runs, the kids to begin to scream out of excitement and chase him. The dog gets fearful and runs into the corner of the room as the kids continue to chase him. As they get near him, in this spare bedroom, he runs past them back down the hallway *to his one place of safety, which is the bedroom where his bed is located.* The kids continue to chase him again into the bedroom and he runs under the bed. Now the kids get down on their knees and start sticking their hands trying to coax the dog out.

I will stop the story right there and let everyone figure out what will probably happen next. I have told this example many times, including in seminars and personal appearances, because it represents the damage a dog that has fear aggression can inflict on a person. When dogs have this kind of personality, and they are put in a situation like this, bad things can happen. We've talked so much about escalation in this book. In this scenario, you can see that there were a number of times things had the opportunity to heighten greatly. So this was not about the kids sticking their hands in a fearful dog's face under the bed. Instead it was all about the series of events that became multiple triggers, and things became worse with every trigger.

- The Past – The family was already dealing with a dog that has a higher prey drive and was naturally reactive.

- The Past – In addition, the dog had already had some serious fear in that he spent the majority of his time in the bedroom in his bed.

- The Past – His bed was his one place of total security.

- Kids came over to the house and, naturally, the environment changed.

- There were things in the house that made the dog even more nervous, like kids running around and screaming.

- A few kids chased the dog down a hallway to an area that was away from his secure bedroom and his bed (it would surprise me if the kids did not get bit at that point).

- The dog gets away from the kids and to his place of security but is followed by the kids.

- Seeing that his bed will not keep him safe from the kids, he does what comes natural in this fearful situation and hides under the bed.

- The kids stick their hands under the bed, and the dog will now play out a *kill or be killed* scenario, which is to bite. Because of the fear, this bite is, most likely, going to be severe.

Now, I want to break down this example because you can see that there were so many opportunities to escalate.

- We know that the bed was his place of security.

- We know that the breed was reactive.

- We know this dog had some serious fear issues.

- Things escalated as the kids came over to the house and made things uncomfortable for the dog.

- Things escalated more as the dog heard the kids screaming and saw them running around.

- Things escalated even more when the kids chased the dog down the hallway.

- Things escalated more as the dog got away from them.

- Things escalated more as the kids chased the dog into the one room in which he felt secure.

- Things escalated more as the dog realized his bed was no longer safe and ran under the bed.

- Things escalated more as the kids stuck their hands under the bed.

- The dog perceived this scenario as his last-ditch effort to stay alive from the people that were trying to do him harm.

- He bites, and because it is a fear aggressive bite, the bite is very severe, or he holds on.

The message here is: please pay attention to your dog's personality. If you own a dog that is a fearful dog, and you are inviting guests over, just be prepared. Remember, this is your dog's home, as well as yours.

Sanctuary Training

In the next chapter, I am going to show you, hopefully, how to get rid of excessive fear and excitement. In dealing with fear, you will learn about using redirection, preventative training, and sanctuary training.

I want to take some time and tell you about another technique called sanctuary training, because it is something that I used a lot in the training of birds earlier in my career as a Hollywood animal trainer. You will learn that sanctuary training is actually used in conjunction with redirection training.

So, here is how it was used differently with each kind of bird:

Pigeons – As an animal trainer on the set in Hollywood, there was a time in the late 1980's when the pigeons I trained for movies, TV shows, and commercials worked nearly every week. They were trained to fly in a number different environments from point A to point B. As a matter of fact, I am sure many of you saw the movie Steel Magnolias. I was in Natchitoches, Louisiana in 1988, and spent a large part of the summer training pigeons for the motion picture.

In the training of pigeons, they normally will fly for seed. When they fly, we use a box about 2'x3' and put about 10–15 birds in the box. We have an identical box with an open top with seed in it. When we release the birds, they are trained to fly to the other box, and we shut it. That all works great, but a way to really get the birds to want to fly to the other box fast is to put another bird in there and let him eat the food. By watching the other bird eat the food, the pigeons are motivated to fly to the box even faster. This is how sanctuary training can work when training pigeons to fly from point A to point B.

Penguins – If we want a penguin to walk from point A to point B, we put a few penguins in another area about 20 feet away. Because penguins are social, and like to be around each other, when the one penguin is released, he will walk to where the other penguins are. I think it is hilarious because the entire crew on the set thinks you are the smartest person in the world. This another way that sanctuary training works.

Seagulls – This way is a bit different, in that there is no other bird involved. Most of the time, if someone wanted a seagull to do a particular action, they would want the bird to fly and land on something. A seagull is one of the only wild animals I can catch in the morning, and have it flying and landing on something by the end of the day.

When we train seagulls, we keep a light line on them, so they cannot fly away. We would put something large near them that they can easily stand on like a table. Once the bird is relaxed, I would step back about 20–30 feet from the bird and let him stay there for about five minutes. As I approached the bird, he might try to fly off. As he did, I would just hold onto the line so he could not fly too far. I would then just gently pick him up and release the bird from my hands from about three feet away from the table. Because of the comfort and safety he felt from the table, he would fly to it. Again, I would step back for five to ten minutes. Remember, the longer the bird is on the table away from me, the more reinforcing it is to him.

As the bird begins to understand, I would simply back up and release the bird farther and farther away from the table. At the same time, we would make the table smaller and smaller, until the bird is flying and landing on a small object. Over the course of time, you can see that we would eventually be able to get our shot.

So that is how sanctuary training works with birds. You will see in the next chapter how sanctuary training works nicely with redirection in dealing with dogs that have a fear of people.

All Situations are Different

Any professional dog trainer will tell you that not all situations are ever the same, but you can see that when you are dealing with fear or excitement, things will often have an opportunity to escalate.

In the next chapter, I will show you how you can use redirection and sanctuary training to help you with a dog that has a fear of people, places, or things.

CHAPTER 7

Rituals and Dog Training

Ok, so now you have arrived at the chapter that should help you with training out some of the unwanted behaviors. I spent a lot of time explaining in the previous chapters about why some of these unwanted habits or rituals happen. In this chapter, I am going to show you how to eliminate or extinguish some of these behaviors so, hopefully, they do not escalate or increase.

If you go back to the color spectrum, remember the farther your dog is away from the center, the more challenging things will be, and the closer your dog is to the center of the spectrum, the easier your dog will be to train.

Green and Blue Dogs

If you are dealing with a green dog with some fear or apprehension, your dog most likely has not yet developed a ritual of fear. This means the training should be easier than the training of the blue dog. If you are training a blue dog that has developed fear or anxiety, it is just going to take longer.

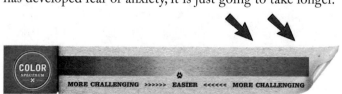

Orange and Red Dogs

If you are working with an orange dog that gets excited over a person, place or thing, just like the green dog, most likely, he has not developed a ritual of excitement.

This means the training should be easier than a red dog. If you are training a red dog that has developed an increased level of excitement from a skateboard or other object, it is going to take longer than the training of the orange dog.

The Training

In dealing with problem solving, there will be four training techniques you might be using. You might use just one of them, you might also use two of them, you might use three of them, or you might use all four of them. Every dog is different, so you need to find out what works for you.

Redirection – Redirection simply means that we redirect our dog away from a person, place, or thing that scares the dog or excites the dog. In my personal experience, redirection works better with fear than it does with excitement. By using redirection, as the name says, you are going to redirect the dog away from that fear with a high-value treat. The biggest mistake I have seen pet owners make is to try to redirect the dog away from something with a treat the dog could care less about. If you want this to work using redirection, it is essential you use something the dog only gets on rare occasions that he loves. This needs to be a high-value treat like chicken, turkey, cheese, beef, or a Bil-Jac treat.

Preventative Training – Preventative training is always coupled with another training technique, so you will never train your dog only using preventative training. Preventative training simply means we are not going to give the dog a chance to be in the situation that starts to manifest that fear. A good example is when someone walks into the house and the dog runs into the bedroom. We obviously want to eliminate that behavior. By giving your dog the opportunity to play out this ritual, it just constantly gets worse. By using preventative training, we would not give the dog the opportunity to be in that situation when guests come over. An example of preventative training in this setting might involve keeping the dog in the back room with the door closed or in a crate in a back room just when guest came over. By doing this, we prevent the dog from playing out that ritual of running in the bedroom.

Corrections – The first two training techniques I just gave you are the techniques I recommend in training the cooler colored dogs. But when I am working with a high-strung dog that really could care less about treats at the moment I am training him, I am going to need to find another technique, and I would use corrections (also called interruptions). I have written this in all my other books, but I always have to explain about corrections to some people that get negative when they hear the word correction.

First of all, there are a number of kinds of corrections. A correction is an interruption, and those interruptions can be a variety of many different things. A great example is in my training sessions when I am teaching a dog (using treats) to sit, stay, lie down, or any advanced behaviors—interruptions are essential. If I am using treats to train a behavior and the dog does not do something right, I will interrupt the dog which means I will put the brakes on and have him stop, and then have him start again With the behavior. That is a correction because it is an interruption.

Another kind of correction might involve a training collar in situations where you are dealing with excitement or using physical corrections. If you are dealing with an orange or red dog and finding a way to get rid of a behavior that comes out of sheer excitement, it would be great to use redirection. Unfortunately, the reality is, redirection will not work in most of these scenarios because the high-value treat you are trying to use is not as great as the dog's desire to seek out what is exciting him.

Sanctuary Training – Sanctuary training will always be used in conjunction with redirection. With sanctuary training, you are removing yourself as a reward to the animal. That, being coupled with giving the dog a reward, can make things that much more reinforcing to the animal.

There are some trainers that will lead you to believe redirection works in every situation, but I am here to tell you, as much as I like using redirection in dealing with fear, in most cases involving extreme excitement, it is not going to work.

Remember that letting dogs play out actions is reinforcing to the dog, so the completion of the bad behavior is the reward. That is why you need to use some kind of training tool to interrupt the behavior. Remember, if he plays out the action, he is rewarded. But if you interrupt the behavior, he does not complete the action and is no longer rewarded.

Now that you have an idea of the kinds of tools we are going to use to get rid of some unwanted behaviors, let's take a look at some of the most common behavior problems that have been allowed to escalate and turn into rituals.

Fear

- Fear of people or a person

- Fear of moving things inside your home

- Fear or excitement of stationary objects

- Afraid to come out of a room

Excitement

- Teaching Slack in Leash

- Jumping on guests/ Counter surfing

- Excitement of moving things inside your home

- Excitement of people, dogs, and moving things outside your home

- Barking & Becoming Reactive (out of excitement)

I am going to start off with dealing with fear, and in the next part of the chapter, I will give you some steps to stop the dog from jumping on people, counter surfing, and getting reactive to a person, place, or thing.

Fear of People

If I take a look at most of the cases of fear I have had to deal with, I would have to say that they came from a fear of people or a person. Allowing things to escalate to a place where this has become a ritual, is not only bad for the dog, but more importantly, fear aggression has the ability to manifest. And the last thing you want to have is that fear aggression directed at a person.

When dealing with a dog where the fear has progressed to the advanced stages, the training must be slow, and be kept positive at all times. If it has escalated to a serious stage, I would highly recommend bringing a professional in who specializes in dealing with this kind of behavior.

The biggest mistake I have seen pet owners make when trying to train dogs with these issues is to move way too fast, and to make the training sessions way too long. The best animal trainers I have met over my career were the ones that took their time in training, so you need to understand that training takes time.

There a lot of variables involved in animal behavior when it comes to fear of people. The first thing you want to find out is whether the dog has a fear of a certain person or a fear of all people. If it is only a certain person or certain people, that is actually much better than being afraid of everyone. If your dog is afraid of pretty much everyone, you can still either eliminate the behavior or decrease the degree of the anxiety, but the training is going to take more time.

Let's start off with dealing with a fear of a certain person, or certain people. There are two methods of training you are going to use to handle this behavior, and they are redirection and sanctuary training.

With redirection you are going to be redirecting the dog away from the person or persons. This means that you will be redirecting with a treat that is greater value to the dog than the fear of the person. That is why it is essential you use a high-value treat. With redirection, you will see that there are many variables that go into the training, but the most important ones are movements, positioning, and lack of eye contact.

With sanctuary training, you have to remember that the dog is most likely uncomfortable around the person of whom he is afraid. Because the dog is afraid of the person, as we redirect the dog, we remove the person from the environment. This makes things even more reinforcing. Here are a few important things to remember before you start training:

When you begin with this behavior, keep the training sessions short: only about two to three minutes if you put in two to three sessions in one day. This means you might only get to step one on day one, but you at least you have a place to start!

We talked about the high-value treat, which means you want to use a treat the dog absolutely goes crazy over, and you want to make sure he only gets this high-value treat during these very short training sessions.

The way I like to begin training a dog that has a fear of a specific person is to start off using a person the dog is *not* afraid of. I always like to teach the dog what I want before I expose the dog to the person, he is afraid of. This is so that the dog understands what we are going to be doing. In the dog's mind, "this is the game."

Movements – You have to remember that the dog most likely is going to be fearful of various movements the person makes, so it is essential that the person try to move as normally as possible. Sometimes people think if they walk slowly, it is better for the dog. That actually can make things worse, because when a person tries to walk slowly, it just looks strange to the dog, so move normally.

Positioning – The way the person is positioned in relationship to the dog has a huge impact as well. If a dog is afraid of a person, having the person simply face the dog can also escalate the fear. So, start off by having the person stand facing away at a 90-degree angle.

Eye Contact – It is imperative that the person we are working with makes no eye contact with the dog. With a lot of dogs that have fear issues, the eye contact really contributes to the animal's fear. Again, think of the person as a "prop."

Giving the Treat – When you have the person give the dog the treat, you want to start off with him standing up. Sometimes kneeling down early on is enough of a movement to scare the dog.

Leash – Always keep the dog on a leash for this type of training.

Now that you have a few tips on what to do, and what not to do, I like to start off by using someone the dog is not afraid of.

- The dog will be on a leash, and the person stands about 15–20 feet away.

- You will walk the dog on the leash to the person.

- The person will face a 90-degree angle away from the dog and will hold a treat between his thumb and forefinger so it is easy for the dog to take.

- Walk the dog to the person's hand where the treat is, and when he gets there, have the person give him the treat, moving his hand and arm as little as possible.

- Repeat this a few times until the dog knows the person is going to give the dog a treat.

Step One

Now that the dog understands how to do this with a person he knows, take the dog away, and repeat the exact same thing with a person the dog is afraid of.

- Again, the dog will be on a leash, and the person will stand about 15–20 feet away.

- You will start by walking the dog with you on the leash to the person. This time the dog might walk a bit slower and a bit more cautiously.

- Again, the person will face a 90-degree angle away from the dog and will hold a treat between his thumb and forefinger so it is easy for the dog to take. He might need to slightly bend over so the dog can take the treat easier.

- Walk the dog to the person's hand where the treat is, and when he gets there, have the person give him the treat, again moving his hand and arm as little as possible.

- Make sure the person always removes himself from the area after he rewards the dog. This is the sanctuary part of the training. You also want to wait a few minutes before you try it again.

- Repeat this a few times until the dog knows the person is going to give the dog a treat.

- With the next few steps, the only changes are going to be the position of the person who the dog is afraid of.

Step Two

When the dog walks at normal speed to the person, does not hesitate, and takes the treat, you are ready to move to Step Two. With this step, the only difference is that we are going rotate the person so that he now faces the direction that you and the dog are coming from. Make sure that the person who now faces the dog, *does not make eye contact* at this time. Repeat the same things you did in Step One.

Step Three

When the dog is consistent, the next step is to have the person kneel down and repeat those same steps.

Step Four

When the dog understands, have the person kneel down as the dog approaches, so the dog sees body movement as he approaches the person.

Step Five

The next step is to change the location. Repeat the same action, but just do everything in a different place.

Step Six

When the dog understands, we want to create more movement from the person the dog has a fear of. This is accomplished by having the person take two slow small steps away from the dog, as he keeps his hand down that is holding the treat. As the dog meets him, he immediately gives the dog a treat.

You can see that by this time, the dog will to start to look more comfortable around this person. The behavior is, by no means trained, but by this time you should start to see a decrease in fear towards the person.

Step Seven

This next step is simply having the person walk even a few more steps, and always finish up with rewarding the dog. Repeat by adding more steps.

Step Eight

Up to now we had the dog walk to the person on a leash. This next step involves the dog and person meeting. This means they will start from about 20 feet away from each other and meet in the middle. You should start to see a difference in your dog's body language, in relationship to the person.

As things start to progress to this stage, you can begin to do things like change locations. You can also have the person start to walk with you and the dog, rewarding the dog periodically. You can also start to bring the person into the house with the dog and start to drop the leash, allowing the dog to come to the person.

As mentioned earlier in the book, the foundation is everything in dog training. It does not matter whether you are training your dog to sit or whether you are dealing with a dog that is afraid of people. You always need to have a place to start and spend a lot of time at that first step. The first step was having the person reward the dog while facing away. So again, when you start with this behavior, keep the training sessions short to only about two to three minutes. It means you might only get to step one on day one with some dogs, but at least you have a place to start!

Fear or Excitement of Moving Objects Inside Your Home

In the training of dogs, to rid themselves of the fear of moving objects, you need to ask yourself a number of questions first. Is the object the dog is afraid of inside or outside the house? The reason is, there are fewer moving objects inside the house that the dog probably will be afraid of. Most of the time it's narrowed down to things like the vacuum cleaner. You can use the same technique I use for the vacuum cleaner with any other moving object inside the house.

Remember, earlier in the book, I talked about multiple triggers, and the vacuum cleaner has probably more triggers than any other behavior you are going to deal with.

Vacuum cleaners can not only bring out fear, but also excitement from your dog. This is why this behavior problem is not color specific. If you have a dog that is afraid or gets excited around vacuum cleaners, to continue vacuuming will most likely increase the excitement or fear in your dog. A green dog can go blue, and an orange dog can go red. I talked earlier about sounds and movements, and mentioned when you are dealing with both, it is often more challenging. With vacuum cleaners there are a number of multiple triggers that involve both sound and movement, so let's take a look:

- What happens before you start to vacuum with the vacuum cleaner? You turn it on.

- What happens before you turn it on? You plug it in.

- What happens before you plug it in? You let the cord out.

- What happens before you let the cord out? You bring it to an area.

- What happens before you bring it to an area? You take it out of the closet.

- What happens before you bring it out of the closet? You open the closet door.

So, as you can see, there are a total of six different triggers that occur long before you actually start to vacuum. Before we begin, I want to remind you to make sure you use the highest valued treat you can use. This is something special the dog only gets at times like this.

You will use redirection for this behavior, as well as sanctuary training. Also, you will to want to keep the training sessions short to about two to three minutes. So, we always want to start off with the very first trigger, and that is to open the door to the closet.

Step One

Your dog will be loose, and I would have the dog follow you to the closet the vacuum cleaner is inside. Give the dog a treat *before* you open the door, so that we start "the game."

Step Two

Repeat what you just did, but now open the door. Do not go in, but reward the dog.

Step Three

Repeat what you just did, but now open the door, go in, and walk to the vacuum cleaner, but do not touch it, and reward the dog.

Step Four

Repeat what you just did, but now open the door, go inside, take the vacuum cleaner out of the closet, put it down, and reward the dog.

Step Five

Repeat what you just did, but now open the door, take the vacuum cleaner out, and take it to the closest outlet, put it down, and reward the dog.

With these next steps, you might to see a slight or increased level of fear or excitement, so you might need to stay at this stage for a while until the dog is calm and relaxed.

Step Six

As the vacuum cleaner is standing there, unwind the cord, and reward your dog. If your dog was okay with that, move onto the next step. If he was not, repeat this until he is okay with you unwinding the cord.

Step Seven

Unwind the cord, and plug it in. If your dog is okay with that, reward him, and move onto the next step. If he is not, repeat this until he is okay with you plugging in the vacuum cord.

Step Eight

With this next step, you will keep the machine unplugged. You will turn the switch to "on." You are now helping your dog get used to hearing that sound. You might need to spend a few sessions at this phase, as the dog is normally conditioned to hearing the vacuum cleaner come on after you turn the switch on.

Step Nine

This next step is where you will turn on the vacuum, but when you do so, you need to literally turn it off right after you turned it on. You should turn it off as fast as you turned it on. You might need to repeat this a few times, as you are conditioning your dog to hearing this sound for a split second, and then reward him. Once your dog is okay with that, you can start to increase it to one full second before you turn it off and reward him. When your dog is okay with that, just start to increase it more and more. Eventually he will learn to be okay with you turning it on, and just listening to the sound.

Although you have made some good progress, the behavior is still not trained, as we have to deal with sounds and movements. By this point, you have done a good job with the sounds, but you now will focus on movement. Also at this stage, you can see your dog most likely is starting to figure out "the game," as we talked about in earlier in the book. He really should get into this training as well!

Step Ten

In this next step, your vacuum cleaner will be plugged in, but not powered on. Start to move it as if you are vacuuming, but only start with six-inch movements, and reward your dog. If your dog is okay, then go to one-foot movements, and reward him. If he is okay with that, you can start to move the vacuum cleaner more and more until you are doing the exact same action as you would do when actually vacuuming. When you can do that, you can move to the last and final step.

Step Eleven

In this last step, you will combine the sound with movement. You will power on the vacuum cleaner, and you will just barely move it, and reward your dog. If he is okay with that, you can start to move it a little more. As in the previous step, you will slowly start to move more and more. Eventually you will get to a place where you are vacuuming, and once this happens you will have trained your dog to get used to the vacuum cleaner using redirection!

Remember every dog is different, and they all learn at different speeds. Once you teach this behavior, you can use these same steps to get your dog used to a variety of other moving things.

Fear of Stationary Objects

When something is stationary that the dog has a fear of, the good news is that the object is stationary and does not move. Much like training dogs that are afraid of people, it is essential the object is introduced to the dog as a "prop," as well. You will want to use a high-value treat the dog only gets in these training sessions.

As with all training sessions that involve redirection, you will want to keep the training sessions to about two to three minutes.

Step One

Start off with the object set on the ground and place a high-value treat about six inches away. Walk the dog over to the object, letting him make his way to the treat. It is very important you do not pull him, as he must make his own decisions in this kind of training. If you can show him where the treat is, that can help too! I would repeat the same thing a few more times and end the session. You do not want to progress to the next step until the dog walks at a good pace to get the treat from the ground.

Step Two

Repeat what you did, and as you get to the object, reach for it and touch it. If your dog is okay with that, let him see the treat on the ground, and let him eat it. I would repeat the same thing a few more times and again end the session.

Step Three

Repeat what you did, and as you get to the object, this time, as you reach for it, pick it up a few inches and put it down. Let your dog take the treat from the ground and eat it. I would repeat the same thing a few more times and end the session.

As you can see, you have built a foundation in which you reach and pick up the object, and the dog gets rewarded for that. As you progress, you will simply lift the object a bit higher each time.

The goal is to pick it up and hold it, and then put it down. That might last a few sessions. The next step would be to pick up the object and walk with it, and again, reward the dog.

By this time, the dog should start getting used to the object.

Fear of Not Wanting to Come Out of the Room

I am going to bring up one last scenario, and this one I actually dealt with about six years ago. It was related to an 11-year-old Aussie mix that was afraid of nearly everything, with the exception of her two owners.

I have handled this problem before, but not to the degree of fear this particular dog had. She had such a fear, she would not even come out of the bedroom. She had a little bed in the corner next to the owner's bed. As a matter of fact, they told me she was so afraid she rarely came out, even when I was not there. And because this had happened for such a long period of time, it had become a ritual of fear.

Because this dog was afraid of everybody and everything, obviously she had multiple triggers. So here is how I trained this dog to come out of the room.

For this, I used solely redirection as the form of technique. The first thing to do is find a high-value treat, as we always do in redirection. I also couple this with sanctuary training. Remember, with sanctuary training, you remove yourself from the dog as an additional reinforcement. Also keep the training sessions to no longer than one minute.

Step One

You want to start off by walking into the room where the dog is, stop about three to four feet from the dog, and toss a treat in front of the dog. If the dog eats the treat, I would do that a few more times, and leave. Always make sure you remove yourself each time from the area as that secondary reinforcement to the dog.

Step Two

Repeat what you did, although I would get a bit closer to the dog as you toss the treat. If the dog eats the treat, I would do that same thing just a few more times and leave the room. I would repeat this step for the next three to four training sessions.

Step Three

At this time, you might start to see the dog get up from his bed, and maybe just stand there. If that happens, you are making some slow, but great progress! Walk to the dog and toss a treat. Repeat that a few more times and leave the room.

Step Four

Now, what you are looking for, is for the dog to take a step or two off his bed. If that happens, again, you are making progress! Walk to the dog and toss a treat. Repeat that a few more times and leave.

Step Five

The next step is to hope the dog will start to move a bit closer to the door each time you walk into the room. If that happens, just reward the dog each time and toss a treat. Repeat that a few more times and leave.

After a few days, you might see the dog start to want to meet you down the hallway. Again, walk to the dog and reward the dog. At this time, the dog might even start to take a treat directly from your hand. Repeat it a few more times. Something else I would do at this time is walk with the dog back to the room and give the dog a treat for going in there. It's great, because it is something most dogs at this point are not expecting. It catches the dog off guard and is a great reward!

What you will see is the dog coming farther and farther down the hallway, and every time the dog comes to you, reward the dog. Now the dog is getting to a point where he takes it upon himself and initiates coming to you. Once that happens, you are well on your way to teaching this dog to get over that fear of not coming out of a room.

Don't forget to remove yourself from the area each time, as the sanctuary training is such a huge part of dealing with fear of people.

Excitement and Reactive Dogs

In this last part of this chapter, I want to show you how to deal with dogs that get reactive or get overly excited. These will be the orange and red dogs. There is an exercise I like to do with dogs that are reactive prior to being trained, and it has to do with calming down a reactive dog.

Teaching Slack in Leash

The exercise I am going to show you is the same one I use in all my dog trainer certification course classes when I am dealing with dogs that are reactive. We actually have done this exercise dozens of times with untrained dogs in animal shelters and humane societies.

The first thing I recommend is to have your favorite training collar on your dog. If you do not have one, I would recommend my Alternative Training Collar, which is an alternative to a choke chain. You want to use a collar that will release nicely, because most importantly, you want to use these sessions to teach the dog to understand you will keep slack in the leash.

I know we've discussed short two to three-minute training sessions a lot in this book, but because we are not necessarily teaching a dog to do a behavior, the sessions can be anywhere from 10–20 minutes.

I would recommend not using treats or any other reinforcement other than petting your dog. If you do use a reinforcement for this, you want to do it every few minutes when he does what you want.

The way I teach the dog is to start off by keeping him next to my leg. What he will learn is that he can do certain things, but there are some things he cannot do. He cannot pull, lunge, or jump. However, he can sit, stand, lie down, and lean against you. Most importantly, every time there is tension in the leash, he is lightly corrected. It is essential that if the dog pulls three to four inches, he is corrected and brought back to the spot where he was, and you release. The reason for this is because if you correct early, at only three to four inches, the dog is rational. And if the dog is rational, the correction is minimal. When you correct your dog, you always want to correct, and release, so that there is slack in the leash. This way the dog is always either standing, sitting, or lying down with slack in the leash.

The greatest part about this behavior is it teaches your dog to understand on his own, what slack in the leash is. Once your dog understands, you are going to find it gives you a lot of control. This is a great ritual the dog can learn very quickly.

Another great thing about teaching this behavior is that it lays a great foundation for the heel, because the heel starts in this exact same position. If the dog is not pulling as you go to train the heel, it will make the beginning of training of the heel that much easier.

Jumping on Guests & Counter Surfing

You have heard me say in this book, as well as chapter nine in my *More What Color is Your Dog?* book, "the completion of the behavior is a reward." When we talk about bad behaviors like jumping on guests or counter surfing, those are the best examples of what goes on in your dog's head.

If you think about the act of jumping on guests, you have to take few steps back and ask why did the dog jump? We do not know exactly, but there is a good possibility it had to do with excitement and the dog wanting to get closer to the person's face. By letting the dog complete that action, he is actually rewarded. This is why I think it is bizarre that some dog trainers tell people to turn their back, and just ignore the dog. Because allowing your dog to play out actions is reinforcing to your dog.

In order to start training this behavior, I would recommend using your favorite training tool. When teaching the dog to not counter surf, or not jump up on people, you need to send a message to your dog that once his feet come off the ground, he is corrected. By doing this, the message you send to your dog is that he is corrected for the feet coming off the ground, and not necessarily putting his feet up on the counter or a person. The reason for this is because if the dog's feet are already up on the counter or person, the dog is most likely going to be less rational. If the dog is less rational, the corrections are going to be more severe. If the front feet are barely coming off the ground, and you correct the dog, the corrections are going to be much more minimal because the dog is a lot more rational.

You will find you will spend more time correcting your dog for jumping on people at the front door than correcting your dog for counter surfing. So, we are going to start off by training dogs not to jump on people.

Earlier in the book, we talked about triggers, and there are a few triggers that happen before your guest actually comes in the house, and there are some triggers that can escalate your dog's reactiveness and excitement level. Triggers, like knocking on doors, doorbells and people talking in high-pitched voices, can both have an effect on increasing your dog's excitement level before sometime comes in.

You certainly cannot get rid of every trigger, but I would recommend you try to eliminate triggers that increase your dog's energy level. So, my suggestion would be to start off by telling everyone you know who is coming over to your house to knock on the door and not use the doorbell. I would also ask them to try their best to just ignore the dog, and not do things that will increase the dog's energy level.

I would start off by putting your dog's leash attached to your favorite collar near the front door, so it is easy to get to.

- What will happen first is the person will knock on the door. This will be a trigger and increase your dog's excitement level.

- He will run to the door.

- As he gets to the door, you want to immediately put on the leash and collar, so this way, you have control. You are now ready to have the person come in.

Step One

Put the leash and collar on the dog. Open the door, and let the person come in just a few feet. If your dog goes to jump up, correct your dog as the front feet barely come off the ground. I would have the person go back out the door and repeat this six to eight times. After that, by no means will your dog be trained, but he should have a good idea of what you are doing.

Step Two

Repeat what you did in step one. Open the door, and let the person come in just a few feet. You should see, sometime during this session, that your dog seems to be jumping less, so you are correcting less. If that happens, you are ready for step three. I would also begin to use any word you like as the dog approaches the person, to calm him down before you correct him. This word is going to be used as a reminder. Some of the words you might want to use might be, "be easy," "easy," or "stay down." You might have your own word.

Step Three

Repeat what you did in step two a few times. The next step is to do the same thing, but this time, as the person comes in, drop the leash. If you see that your dog does not jump with the leash dragging, you are ready for step four. Make sure you always say your word or words as the dog approaches the person.

Step Four

Repeat what you did in step three a few times. The next step is to do the same thing, but this time, the dog will have on only a training collar and no leash. If your dog is good with that, you can then take off the training collar, and the behavior is trained. You are going to find the word you use is really a big help at this point, as well.

This is a great technique that I have used for over four decades. Take your time. You might find you need to stay at a certain step or phase for two or three days. There is absolutely nothing wrong with that. You might also find you need to regress, and take a few steps back, which happens sometimes as well.

Dogs Reactive to Moving Objects Outside

I think that this might be one of the most common, and at the same time, potentially dangerous behavioral problems. When a dog is reactive to something moving, the dog could get hurt, and also seriously injure the person that is in or on the object.

I will show you a technique that I use with dogs that are reactive to skateboards. With this particular action the dog plays out, there are multiple triggers, and they are both sight and sound related. The dog will hear the skateboard before he sees it, so that sound is the first trigger. The next trigger and escalation will come from the visual excitement from the moving object. As the skateboard goes from left to right, or vice-versa, that increases things more.

In the training of this behavior, you will be using redirection using a high-value treat, and possibly some smaller corrections or interruptions.

Step One

The very first thing you want to do is to have the person hold a skateboard, walk up to the dog, and then reward the dog with a treat. I would repeat that same thing three to four times. We talked about "the game" in chapter three, and we want the dog to know *this* is the game.

Step Two

The next step is to start off doing the same thing as step one a few times. The third time have the person walk up to the dog and put the skateboard down. Then have him pick it up and reward the dog.

Step Three

Next, you want to repeat step two, still staying right near the dog, but when the skateboarder puts the skateboard down, have him move it slowly a few inches back and forth with his foot, and reward the dog. He can smell it if he likes, as long as he is not becoming reactive and chasing it. You might need to stay at this step for a few sessions until you get to a point where the dog just ignores the skateboard.

Step Four

Repeat step three, but when the person puts down the skateboard, have him move the skateboard a few feet this time, and you and he, reward the dog. Repeat that a few times.

Step Five

Repeat step four, but when he puts down the skateboard, have him start to roll it away from him. At this point, I would just spend a lot of time rolling it around, sending the skateboard in different directions. At the same time, you and he always reward the dog.

Step Six

Repeat step five, but when the person puts down the skateboard, have him stand on it. Repeat that a few times, and if the dog is okay with that, have the person step off of the skateboard, and push it with his foot away from him, creating the same skateboard action as step five. Again, both of you reward the dog.

Step Seven

Repeat step six, but when the person puts down the skateboard, have him stand on it, and slowly push it only a foot or two, as he rides on it. Repeat that a few times, and I would spend a lot of time at this step for a few sessions, always rewarding the dog as the person gets off the skateboard.

You can see how we started and progressed to this last stage. Once you are at this stage of the behavior, the person on the skateboard can simply start to go a bit faster each day, and also move farther away from the dog as well.

We talked about the game in chapter three. I cannot think of something that defines what "the game" is more than the training of this behavior. This behavior is also the best example of using redirection in training too. Take it slow!

Dogs Becoming Reactive Out of Excitement

This technique is saved for last because it is really one of the most important ones.

You might own a dog that gets very excited in his home, when certain people or other dogs walk by. You might also own a dog that gets excited on walks, and it might seem that being on the leash makes it even worse when he gets excited. That excitement might even escalate into your dog pulling, lunging, and barking.

We have talked this about in the book: as minimal as the pulling, lunging, or barking might be initially, allowing the dog to play out and complete the action is reinforcing to your dog. Because he is allowed to play out the action, the behavior will likely escalate over time. As that happens unwanted rituals are created.

So, whether it is a situation where your dog gets excited in your home or outside your home, you need to find a way to interrupt the action.

Throughout this chapter, I have spent a lot of time showing you how to use redirection as a great way to deal with issues that involve fear and excitement. But with the level of excitement the dog is showing, which is totally different than with fear, you are going to need to find a way to interrupt the action your dog wants to play out. I say the word "want" because it is essential you interrupt the behavior before it actually happens, so timing is essential.

How is this done? It is accomplished by starting off with the help of your favorite training collar. The first thing you want to do is find a place where your dog does not get excited with the thing that makes him get excited. That is the most important thing you want to do, because when you find this place, that distance from the dog or person is where you start. The place I am talking about is a place where the dog does not even look at the person or animal that excites him.

This means that if your dog gets reactive and excited inside the house, you want to start with the person or animal that excites the dog all the way across the street, or a place where the dog does not care about the person or animal. It also means if you train your dog outside, stay back at a place far enough where the dog does not react to the person or animal. You will see that your initial position is the key.

By discovering these things, it now gives you a place to start, and you certainly know what your goal is too, and that is to get the dog next to the person or animal without becoming reactive.

If you are outside and the dog is on a leash, start off with your dog in that place where he is not distracted by the person or animal. Take a step toward the person or animal that gets him excited and watch his attitude. If there is no change, take another step. *What you are looking for is just a glance from your dog at the distraction.* If your dog glances, correct him with the collar, and guide him back to you. If you are far away from the distraction, because the dog is rational, the correction should be minimal. Remember:

- If it becomes a stare or the dog becomes agitated, you moved too close, and I would go back to the original location.

- What you are looking for is the dog to just glance at the person or animal. Once the dog glances, correct the dog with the training collar you are using, and guide the dog back to you.

At this point you might want to use a treat or something that is not too high-value. Also if you use a treat, and your dog does become more excited about the treat, I would put the treat away. The reason for this is you don't want the dog concerned more about the treat than the distraction. It is essential that we deal with the distraction and teach the dog not to become reactive.

So the goal in teaching this technique is not to allow your dog to fixate or stare at the person or animal. You now have a place to start, and you are simply going to spend a lot of time at the place where the dog is not reactive. Take a step forward each day and do the same thing with your dog. If the dog glances, correct the dog, say your dog's name, and he should come to you.

Over time, you can see that the dog actually becomes conditioned to not allow himself to even look at the person or animal. If you start with this behavior from a distance, and slowly move toward the dog each day, you simply do not let your dog get conditioned to allow himself to look at the distraction.

Remember, if your dog is able to look at the distraction, that is the beginning of the escalation. It begins with a glance, which we correct. But if the glance is not corrected, it escalates into fixating. If the dog is allowed to fixate, he will then take it to the next level with lunging or barking. And things will escalate from there.

Once your dog is trained using this technique with one distraction, you can use the same technique with any other distraction. So just find the place your dog is okay with a distraction and start from there.

Closing

I really hope you got a lot out of this book. Feel free to pick it up and re-read parts of it if there are certain techniques that I have demonstrated that relate to the training you use with your dog.

Dog training is all about starting off with getting to know and understand your dog. Once you have an understanding of your dog's personality and attitude, you can start to train him. Remember the color spectrum too, and don't forget your dog can change colors based on the environment he is in, and the distractions that are introduced in that environment.

Dog training is also about having a goal and game plan. You need to have a starting line and a finish line in mind for that training session, as small as it may be. By having a game plan, and also having an idea of what your final goal is, you can then begin to train your dog one step at a time. The biggest mistake you can make is not having a game plan.

In closing, I just wanted to say how great my life has been as a professional dog trainer for over 40 years. Performing in live shows in every theme park in Southern California with the exception of Disneyland in my twenties was just an awesome experience. Working as a Hollywood dog trainer for decades, authoring five books, hosting two nationally syndicated TV series, doing personal appearances, and selling 500,000 dog training DVDs is nothing short of a blessing.

The reason I chose a dog training career is because I love dogs and find that when you take the time to build that unconditional bond and trust, training becomes a blast for both you and the dog!

Happy Training!

For more information on Joel Silverman's Dog Trainer Certification courses, personal appearances, or his Alternative Training Collar, please check out his website at www.joelsilverman.net.

Credits

Joel Silverman and Animal Consultants International Inc. wish to thank Dreamstime.com for making these photos available for this book! We thought it was appropriate to give credit to the individuals that submitted the photos to Dreamstime.com. for use.

Figure 1 - ID 63527222 © Chris Cross | Dreamstime.com – Dog Gnawing on Toy

Figure 2 - ID 10794190 © Stef Bennett | Dreamstime.com – JRT

Figure 9 - ID 155342059 © Eva Blanco | Dreamstime.com – The Game

Figure 10 - ID 139772848 © Gloria Anderson | Dreamstime.com – Lab Chasing Frisbee

Figure 11 - ID 52078470 © Maxwell De Araujo Rodrigues | Dreamstime.com – Border Collie

Figure 12 - ID 26302909 © Ryan Simpson | Dreamstime.com – Boxer

Figure 13 - ID 17501107 © Viktoria Makarova | Dreamstime.com – Golden Retriever

Figure 14 ID 143775178 © Alexander Bogdanovich | Dreamstime.com – Westie

Figure 15 - ID 163991320 © Dominika Petrlikova | Dreamstime.com – Aussie in Air

Figure 16 - ID 55989624 © Bigandt | Dreamstime.com – Malinois Profile

Figure 17 - ID 104387989 © NonoandJessi | Dreamstime.com -Malinois Laying Down

Figure 18 - ID 137131455 © Sarit Richerson | Dreamstime.com – Dog Tugging on toy

Figure 19 - ID 89584874 © William Wise | Dreamstime.com – Hound Chewing on Bone

Figure 20 - ID 113750784 © Ryhor Bruyeu | Dreamstime.com – Police dog toy

Figure 21 - ID 77058789 © Annaav | Dreamstime.com – Shepherd Starting

Figure 22 - ID 76188268 © Ryhor Bruyeu | Dreamstime.com – Dog Biting Sleeve

Figure 23 - ID 70290307 © Ryhor Bruyeu | Dreamstime.com – Dog Carrying Sleeve

Figure 24 - ID 10728936 © Nikolai Tsvetkov | Dreamstime.com – Dog Laying with Sleeve

Figure 25 - ID 89203426 © Chinook203 | Dreamstime.com – Dog biting bite suit

Other Books by Joel Silverman

More What Color is Your Dog?
by Joel Silverman

Proven techniques to work with your dog, as defined through dog personality color descriptions.

https://doceblantstore.com/collections/how-to/products/
more-what-color-is-your-dog

**Bond with Your Heart;
Train with Your Brain**
By Joel Silverman

Learn to bond with your pets and get to know them, developing a relationship based on trust.

https://doceblantstore.com/collections/how-to/products/
bond-with-your-heart-train-with-your-brain